THIS BOOK BELONGS TO

Abigail Butler

START DATE

June 25, 2024

SHE READS TRUTH

FOUNDERS

FOUNDER
Raechel Myers

CO-FOUNDER
Amanda Bible Williams

EXECUTIVE

CHIEF EXECUTIVE OFFICER
Ryan Myers

CHIEF OPERATING OFFICER
Mark D. Bullard

EDITORIAL

MANAGING EDITOR
Lindsey Jacobi, MDiv

PRODUCTION EDITOR
Hannah Little, MTS

ASSOCIATE EDITOR
Kayla De La Torre, MAT

COPY EDITOR
Becca Owens, MA

CREATIVE

SENIOR ART DIRECTOR
Annie Glover

DESIGN MANAGER
Kelsea Allen

ART DIRECTOR
Lauren Haag

DESIGNER
Ashley Phillips

MARKETING

MARKETING DIRECTOR
Whitney Hoffmann

GROWTH MARKETING MANAGERS
Katie Bevels
Blake Showalter

PRODUCT MARKETING MANAGER
Krista Squibb

CONTENT MARKETING STRATEGIST
Tameshia Williams, ThM

MARKETING PROJECT COORDINATOR
Kyndal Kearns

OPERATIONS

OPERATIONS DIRECTOR
Allison Sutton

OPERATIONS MANAGER
Mary Beth Steed

GROUP SALES AND
ENGAGEMENT SPECIALIST
Karson Speth

OPERATIONS ASSISTANT
Emily Andrews

SHIPPING

SHIPPING MANAGER
Marian Byne

FULFILLMENT LEAD
Kajsa Matheny

FULFILLMENT SPECIALISTS
Kimberly Cannon
Kelsey Simpson

COMMUNITY ENGAGEMENT

COMMUNITY ENGAGEMENT SPECIALISTS
Hannah Lamb
Katy McKnight
Heather Vollono

CONTRIBUTORS

ART
Laci Fowler

SPECIAL THANKS
Russ Ramsey, MDiv, ThM
Jessica Lamb
Melanie Rainer
Ellen Taylor
Amanda Barnhart
Emily Knapp
Julie Allen

SUBSCRIPTION INQUIRIES
orders@shereadstruth.com

SHE READS TRUTH™

© 2018, 2024 by She Reads Truth, LLC
All rights reserved. First edition 2018.
Second edition 2024.

All photography used by permission.

ISBN 978-1-962221-03-0

1 2 3 4 5 6 7 8 9 10

All Scripture is taken from the Christian Standard Bible®, Copyright © 2020 by Holman Bible Publishers. Used by permission. Christian Standard Bible® and CSB® are federally registered trademarks of Holman Bible Publishers.

Though the dates, locations, and individuals in this book have been carefully researched, scholars disagree on many of these topics.

Research support provided by Logos Bible Software™. Learn more at logos.com.

This book was printed offset in Nashville, Tennessee, on 70# Lynx Opaque. Cover is 100# Cougar Opaque with a soft touch lamination.

@SHEREADSTRUTH

Download the She Reads Truth app, available for iOS and Android

 Subscribe to the She Reads Truth Podcast

1 & 2 CORINTHIANS

We are many,
but we are one
in Christ.

Amanda

Amanda Bible Williams
CO-FOUNDER

I work with a truly spectacular group of people, and we each bring a different perspective to our roles. We have team members who are fiercely protective of words, watching over details, like comma placement and hyphen length, with laser-like focus. Our creative team will defend the aesthetic integrity of the She Reads Truth brand as long as they have breath, and another teammate has yet to sit through a meeting without bringing to our attention the needs and desires of you, the Shes who read truth with us. We all have different jobs, and sometimes it is our job to disagree.

Early on in working together, back when it was just the two of us, Raechel and I learned a valuable lesson: seeing things differently is a gift to be stewarded, not a tension to be avoided. Today there are many more teammates at SRT headquarters, and this lesson still rings true—each person brings different skills and perspectives to the table, but we are a team. We are here for each other, for the work set before us, and for you. Above all, we are here to hold out God's Word and bring glory to Him. Our differences help, not hinder, this pursuit.

It's easy for me to see God's provision in the differences among our team members. But I'm embarrassed to admit I often expect homogeneity in the Church. I find myself frustrated by our differences, bothered that we can't all agree on every aspect of our faith and life as followers of Jesus. I'm saddened when these differences go beyond disagreements to cause division, and I get discouraged when these divisions are not easily overcome. I forget that God's Word and perfect wisdom are not diminished by our limited understanding or altered by our various opinions.

In his letters to the church at Corinth, the apostle Paul encouraged this congregation of young believers to embrace their common and primary identity in Christ. He desired for them to know and act on the truth that "we were all baptized by one Spirit into one body" (1Co 12:13). The image of the Church as one body appears throughout these letters, making clear Paul's resounding declaration: we are many, but we are one in Christ.

Each map, chart, and theological extra in this Reading Guide was created to equip you to read and understand 1 & 2 Corinthians, both in their original contexts and in how we can understand these instructions in our lives today. Take a close look at the "Spiritual Gifts" infographic, and marvel at God's creativity among His people. Read "The Lord's Supper" chart, and give thanks for this tangible practice.

As you read, ask the Holy Spirit to open your eyes to see the Church all around you. Ask Him to teach you more about Himself, His body of believers, and the truth of His Word. Like the church at Corinth, we come to this text from a colorful array of backgrounds, experiences, and traditions, but we have a Savior who binds us together. May His mercy and grace unite us as we read.

Design
on Purpose

At She Reads Truth, we believe in pairing the inherently beautiful Word of God with the aesthetic beauty it deserves. Each of our resources is thoughtfully and artfully designed to highlight the beauty, goodness, and truth of Scripture in a way that reflects the themes of each curated reading plan.

For this Reading Guide, we have featured artwork by Laci Fowler (see more about her on page 13!), as her work is such a vivid illustration of the kind of church Paul describes in his letters to the Corinthians. These letters remind us that the Church is one body made up of many parts, pointing us to the unity in diversity that is anchored in Christ.

Laci uses loose, organic shapes in bold, textured brush strokes to build her landscapes and florals, and these different shapes work together to make a cohesive picture. Created using mixed mediums like acrylics, oil pastels, and gouache, these art pieces represent many believers coming together as one. We paired a bright green and blue color palette to match the energy and vibrancy of the artwork. These details serve as a reminder of the ways your unique value contributes to the overall beauty and mission of the body of Christ.

HOW TO USE THIS BOOK

She Reads Truth is a community of women dedicated to reading the Word of God every day. In this **1 & 2 Corinthians** reading plan, we will read the books of 1 & 2 Corinthians, along with complementary passages of Scripture, to be strengthened by the gospel as we seek to live together as the unified body of Christ.

READ & REFLECT

Your **1 & 2 Corinthians** book focuses primarily on Scripture, with added features to come alongside your time with God's Word.

SCRIPTURE READING

Designed for a Monday start, this book presents the books of 1 & 2 Corinthians in daily readings, along with additional passages curated to show how the theme of the main reading can be found throughout Scripture.

🔖 *Additional passages are marked in your daily reading with the Going Deeper heading.*

REFLECTION QUESTIONS

Each week features questions and space for personal reflection.

COMMUNITY & CONVERSATION

You can start reading this book at any time! If you want to join women from Indianapolis to Ireland as they read along with you, the She Reads Truth community will start Day 1 of **1 & 2 Corinthians** on Monday, June 24, 2024.

 ## SHE READS TRUTH APP

Devotionals corresponding to each daily reading can be found in the **1 & 2 Corinthians** reading plan on the She Reads Truth app. Devotionals will be published each weekday once the plan begins on Monday, June 24, 2024. You can use the app to participate in community discussion and more.

GRACE DAY

Use Saturdays to catch up on your reading, pray, and rest in the presence of the Lord.

WEEKLY TRUTH

Sundays are set aside for Scripture memorization.

See tips for memorizing Scripture on page 156.

EXTRAS

This book features additional tools to help you gain a deeper understanding of the text.

Find a complete list of extras on pages 11–12.

 SHEREADSTRUTH.COM

The **1 & 2 Corinthians** reading plan and devotionals will also be available at SheReadsTruth.com as the community reads each day. Invite your family, friends, and neighbors to read along with you!

 SHE READS TRUTH PODCAST

Subscribe to the She Reads Truth Podcast, and join our founders and their guests each week as they talk about what you'll read in the week ahead.

 Podcast episodes 231–236 for our **1 & 2 Corinthians** *series release on Mondays beginning June 24, 2024.*

Table of Contents

One

Two

Three

Four

Six

Five

Featured Artist

LACI FOWLER

Laci is an artist focused on creating original artwork inspired by her life in Middle Tennessee, where she renovated a historic home with her husband and son.

1 Corinthians

God is faithful; you were called by him into fellowship with his Son, Jesus Christ our Lord.

1 CORINTHIANS 1:9

1 Corinthians

TIME TO READ 1 CORINTHIANS

58 Minutes

ON THE TIMELINE

Paul wrote this letter to the Corinthian church during the last year of his three-year ministry at Ephesus, likely a few weeks before Pentecost in the spring of AD 56 (Ac 20:1–6, 31; 1Co 16:8).

A LITTLE BACKGROUND

First Corinthians is actually the second letter Paul wrote to the Corinthian church. His earlier letter to Corinth, which was not included in the canon of Scripture but is referenced in 1 Corinthians 5:9, warned them not to associate with the sexually immoral. The writing of this second letter, 1 Corinthians, was prompted by reports of rivalry within the church (1Co 1:11). Paul addressed this in his letter, along with other troubling issues, including an incestuous relationship among the membership (1Co 5:1), division that arose during observance of the Lord's Supper (1Co 11:18, 20), and confusion over the resurrection of the dead (1Co 15:12). As he was writing this letter to the Corinthian church, it is likely that he received a letter from the church in Corinth asking his opinion on various issues, as he included replies to those concerns as well (1Co 7:1, 25; 8:1; 12:1; 16:1).

MESSAGE & PURPOSE

The main theme of Paul's letter is that Jesus is Lord and believers are His possession. For Paul, whatever issue was discussed, the answer always included a reminder of the Lord's authority over the Church (1Co 1:2, 10). First Corinthians is the most literary of Paul's letters, using stylistic devices like irony, repetition, alliteration, and other wordplays to communicate to his readers the necessity of accepting the Lord's authority.

In addition to motivating the Corinthian church to acknowledge the Lord's ownership, Paul addressed key topics such as Christian unity, morality, spiritual gifts, love, and the resurrection.

GIVE THANKS FOR THE BOOK OF 1 CORINTHIANS

First Corinthians contributes greatly to our understanding of Christian life, ministry, and relationships by showing us how the members of the Church—Christ's body—are to function together. Paul gave specific solutions to specific problems, but the underlying answer to them all is for the Church and its members to live Christ-centered lives.

Thrace

Macedonia

NEAPOLIS

PHILIPPI

AMPHIPOLIS

APOLLONIA

THESSALONICA

BEREA

TROAS

Asia

EPHESUS

ATHENS

CORINTH

CENCHREAE

Crete

Mediterranean Sea

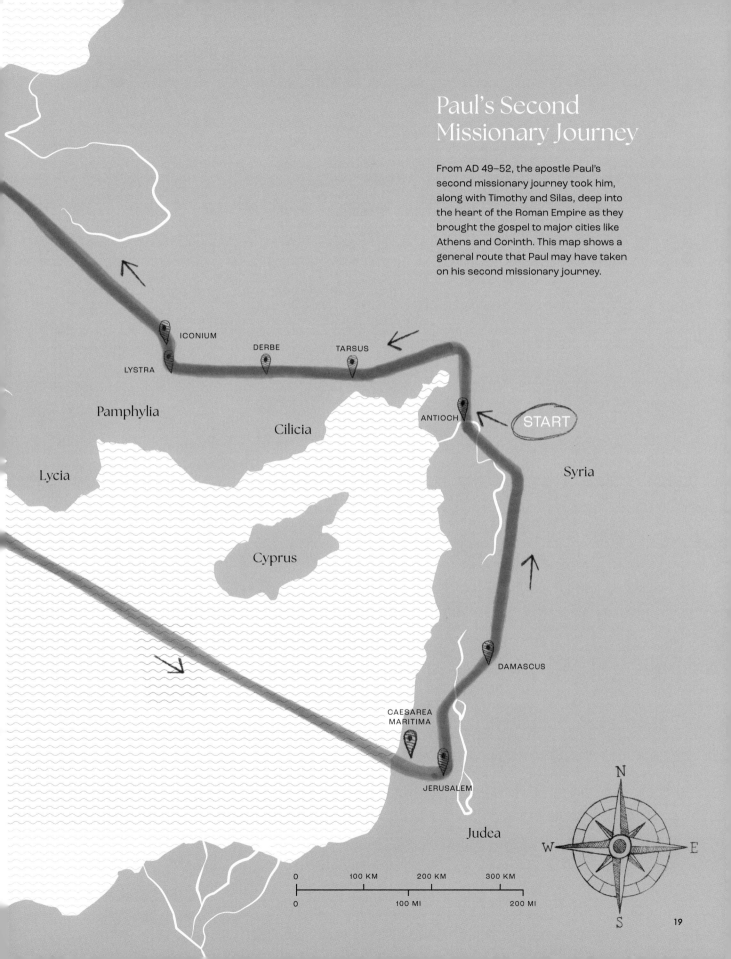

Paul's Second Missionary Journey

From AD 49–52, the apostle Paul's second missionary journey took him, along with Timothy and Silas, deep into the heart of the Roman Empire as they brought the gospel to major cities like Athens and Corinth. This map shows a general route that Paul may have taken on his second missionary journey.

ICONIUM

DERBE

TARSUS

LYSTRA

ANTIOCH

START

Pamphylia

Cilicia

Lycia

Syria

Cyprus

DAMASCUS

CAESAREA MARITIMA

JERUSALEM

Judea

N

W

E

S

0	100 KM	200 KM	300 KM
0		100 MI	200 MI

Week One

Laci Fowler, *Celebrate*, mixed media on canvas, 16x20 in.

Christ, the Power and Wisdom of God

1 Corinthians 1

GREETING

[1] Paul, called as an apostle of Christ Jesus by God's will, and Sosthenes our brother:

[2] To the church of God at Corinth, to those sanctified in Christ Jesus, called as saints, with all those in every place who call on the name of Jesus Christ our Lord—both their Lord and ours.

[3] Grace to you and peace from God our Father and the Lord Jesus Christ.

THANKSGIVING

[4] I always thank my God for you because of the grace of God given to you in Christ Jesus, [5] that you were enriched in him in every way, in all speech and all knowledge. [6] In this way, the testimony about Christ was confirmed among you, [7] so that you do not lack any spiritual gift as you eagerly wait for the revelation of our Lord Jesus Christ. [8] He will also strengthen you to the end, so that you will be blameless in the day of our Lord Jesus

As you read, use the notes section to mark any places that give you insight into life in the Corinthian church, instruction for living as a unified spiritual community, or teachings on how believers are to treat one another as the body of Christ. At the end of each week, there will be space for extended reflection on what you observed in your reading.

Christ. [9] God is faithful; you were called by him into fellowship with his Son, Jesus Christ our Lord.

DIVISIONS AT CORINTH

[10] Now I urge you, brothers and sisters, in the name of our Lord Jesus Christ, that all of you agree in what you say, that there be no divisions among you, and that you be united with the same understanding and the same conviction. [11] For it has been reported to me about you, my brothers and sisters, by members of Chloe's people, that there is rivalry among you. [12] What I am saying is this: One of you says, "I belong to Paul," or "I belong to Apollos," or "I belong to Cephas," or "I belong to Christ." [13] Is Christ divided? Was Paul crucified for you? Or were you baptized in Paul's name? [14] I thank God that I baptized none of you except Crispus and Gaius, [15] so that no one can say you were baptized in my name. [16] I did, in fact, baptize the household of Stephanas; beyond that, I don't recall if I baptized anyone else. [17] For Christ did not send me to baptize, but to preach the gospel—not with eloquent wisdom, so that the cross of Christ will not be emptied of its effect.

CHRIST THE POWER AND WISDOM OF GOD

[18] For the word of the cross is foolishness to those who are perishing, but it is the power of God to us who are being saved.

[19] For it is written,

> I will destroy the wisdom of the wise,
> and I will set aside the intelligence of the intelligent.

[20] Where is the one who is wise? Where is the teacher of the law? Where is the debater of this age? Hasn't God made the world's wisdom foolish? [21] For since, in God's wisdom, the world did not know God through wisdom, God was pleased to save those who believe through the foolishness of what is preached. [22] For the Jews ask for signs and the Greeks seek wisdom, [23] but we preach Christ crucified, a stumbling block to the Jews and foolishness to the Gentiles. [24] Yet to those who are called, both Jews and Greeks, Christ is the power of God and the wisdom of God, [25] because God's foolishness is wiser than human wisdom, and God's weakness is stronger than human strength.

BOASTING ONLY IN THE LORD

[26] Brothers and sisters, consider your calling: Not many were wise from a human perspective, not many powerful, not many of noble birth. [27] Instead, God has chosen what is foolish in the world to shame the wise, and God has chosen what is weak in the world to shame the strong. [28] God has chosen what is insignificant and despised in the world—what is viewed as nothing—to bring to nothing what is viewed as something, [29] so that no one may boast in his presence. [30] It is from him that you are in Christ Jesus, who became wisdom from God for us—our righteousness, sanctification, and redemption— [31] in order that, as it is written: Let the one who boasts, boast in the Lord.

GOING DEEPER

Isaiah 52:13–15

THE SERVANT'S SUFFERING AND EXALTATION

[13] See, my servant will be successful;
he will be raised and lifted up and greatly exalted.
[14] Just as many were appalled at you—
his appearance was so disfigured
that he did not look like a man,
and his form did not resemble a human being—
[15] so he will sprinkle many nations.
Kings will shut their mouths because of him,
for they will see what had not been told them,
and they will understand what they had not heard.

John 1:14–18

[14] The Word became flesh and dwelt among us. We observed his glory, the glory as the one and only Son from the Father, full of grace and truth. [15] (John testified concerning him and exclaimed, "This was the one of whom I said, 'The one coming after me ranks ahead of me, because he existed before me.'") [16] Indeed, we have all received grace upon grace from his fullness, [17] for the law was given through Moses; grace and truth came through Jesus Christ. [18] No one has ever seen God. The one and only Son, who is himself God and is at the Father's side—he has revealed him.

Handwritten notes (right margin):

- Corinthians were divided over a number of teachers (v. 12). But ultimately we are + should be united in Christ!

- Christ crucified is a stumbling block to those w/out faith.
  ↓
  this is so we may only boast in the Lord not in others.

Spiritual Wisdom

1 Corinthians 2

PAUL'S PROCLAMATION

[1] When I came to you, brothers and sisters, announcing the mystery of God to you, I did not come with brilliance of speech or wisdom. [2] I decided to know nothing among you except Jesus Christ and him crucified. [3] I came to you in weakness, in fear, and in much trembling. [4] My speech and my preaching were not with persuasive words of wisdom but with a demonstration of the Spirit's power, [5] so that your faith might not be based on human wisdom but on God's power.

SPIRITUAL WISDOM

[6] We do, however, speak a wisdom among the mature, but not a wisdom of this age, or of the rulers of this age, who are coming to nothing. [7] On the contrary, we speak God's hidden wisdom in a mystery, a wisdom God predestined before the ages for our glory. [8] None of the rulers of this age knew this wisdom, because if they had known it, they would not have crucified the Lord of glory. [9] But as it is written,

What no eye has seen, no ear has heard,
and no human heart has conceived—
God has prepared these things for those
who love him.

[10] Now God has revealed these things to us by the Spirit, since the Spirit searches everything, even the depths of God. [11] For who knows a person's thoughts except his spirit within him? In the same way, no one knows the thoughts of God except the Spirit of God. [12] Now we have not received the spirit of the world, but the Spirit who comes from God, so that we may understand what has been freely given to us by God. [13] We also speak these things, not in words taught by human wisdom, but in those taught by the Spirit, explaining spiritual things to spiritual people. [14] But the person without the Spirit does not receive what comes from God's Spirit, because it is foolishness to him; he is not able to understand it since it is evaluated spiritually. [15] The spiritual person,

however, can evaluate everything, and yet he himself cannot be evaluated by anyone. [16] For

who has known the Lord's mind,
that he may instruct him?

But we have the mind of Christ.

🔖 GOING DEEPER

Proverbs 2:6–10

[6] For the LORD gives wisdom;
from his mouth come knowledge and understanding.
[7] He stores up success for the upright;
He is a shield for those who live with integrity
[8] so that he may guard the paths of justice
and protect the way of his faithful followers.
[9] Then you will understand righteousness, justice,
and integrity—every good path.
[10] For wisdom will enter your heart,
and knowledge will delight you.

Romans 8:26–30

[26] In the same way the Spirit also helps us in our weakness, because we do not know what to pray for as we should, but the Spirit himself intercedes for us with inexpressible groanings. [27] And he who searches our hearts knows the mind of the Spirit, because he intercedes for the saints according to the will of God.

[28] We know that all things work together for the good of those who love God, who are called according to his purpose. [29] For those he foreknew he also predestined to be conformed to the image of his Son, so that he would be the firstborn among many brothers and sisters. [30] And those he predestined, he also called; and those he called, he also justified; and those he justified, he also glorified.

all we need is Christ crucified!
↓
this wisdom is revealed to us by the Spirit!
↓
The Spirit is given to us by God.
✱ the Holy Spirit helps us rightly understand God's design.

our salvation is completely a work of God & Him alone!

God the Spirit

The following series of questions and answers from the "God the Spirit" catechism in the *Book of Common Prayer* offer clarity about the person and work of the Holy Spirit.

What is the Holy Spirit?

The Holy Spirit is the Third Person of the Trinity, God at work in the world and in the Church even now.

JB 32:8; MT 28:19; LK 3:22; JN 14:25–26; 1JN 5:6–8

How is the Holy Spirit revealed in the Old Covenant?

The Holy Spirit is revealed in the Old Covenant as the giver of life, the One who spoke through the prophets.

GN 1:1–2; JB 33:4; PS 104:30; IS 61:1–3; EZK 2:2; 11:5; JL 2:28

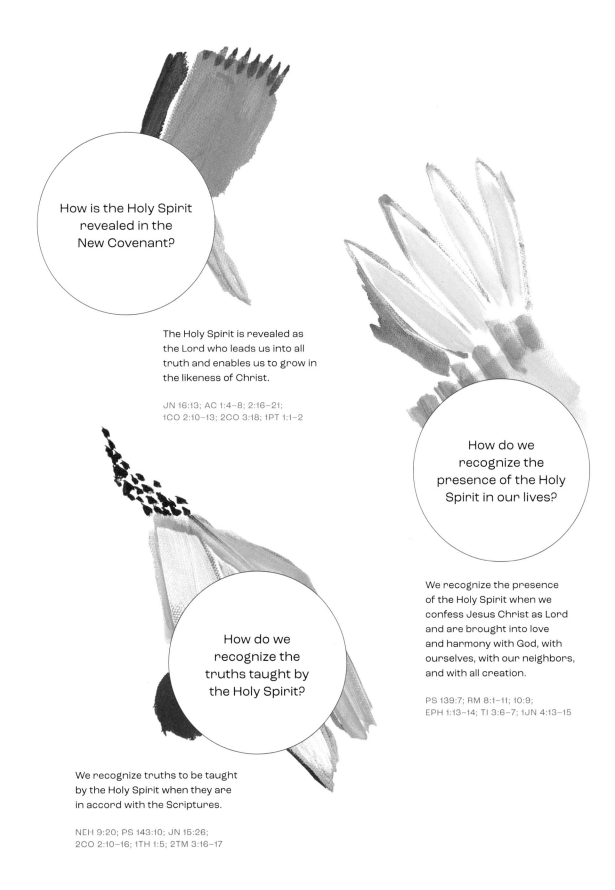

How is the Holy Spirit revealed in the New Covenant?

The Holy Spirit is revealed as the Lord who leads us into all truth and enables us to grow in the likeness of Christ.

JN 16:13; AC 1:4–8; 2:16–21; 1CO 2:10–13; 2CO 3:18; 1PT 1:1–2

How do we recognize the presence of the Holy Spirit in our lives?

We recognize the presence of the Holy Spirit when we confess Jesus Christ as Lord and are brought into love and harmony with God, with ourselves, with our neighbors, and with all creation.

PS 139:7; RM 8:1–11; 10:9; EPH 1:13–14; TI 3:6–7; 1JN 4:13–15

How do we recognize the truths taught by the Holy Spirit?

We recognize truths to be taught by the Holy Spirit when they are in accord with the Scriptures.

NEH 9:20; PS 143:10; JN 15:26; 2CO 2:10–16; 1TH 1:5; 2TM 3:16–17

Christ, Our Foundation

1 Corinthians 3

THE PROBLEM OF IMMATURITY

¹ For my part, brothers and sisters, I was not able to speak to you as spiritual people but as people of the flesh, as babies in Christ. ² I gave you milk to drink, not solid food, since you were not yet ready for it. In fact, you are still not ready, ³ because you are still worldly. For since there is envy and strife among you, are you not worldly and behaving like mere humans? ⁴ For whenever someone says, "I belong to Paul," and another, "I belong to Apollos," are you not acting like mere humans?

THE ROLE OF GOD'S SERVANTS

⁵ What then is Apollos? What is Paul? They are servants through whom you believed, and each has the role the Lord has given. ⁶ I planted, Apollos watered, but **God gave the growth.** ⁷ So, then, neither the one who plants nor the one who waters is anything, but only God who gives the growth. ⁸ Now he who plants and he who waters are one, and each will receive his own reward according to his own labor. ⁹ For we are God's coworkers. You are God's field, God's building.

¹⁰ According to God's grace that was given to me, I have laid a foundation as a skilled master builder, and another builds on it. But each one is to be careful how he builds on it. ¹¹ For no one can lay any foundation other than what has been laid down. **That foundation is Jesus Christ.** ¹² If anyone builds on the foundation with gold, silver, costly stones, wood, hay, or straw, ¹³ each one's work will become obvious. For the day will disclose it, because it will be revealed by fire; the fire will test the quality of each one's work. ¹⁴ If anyone's work that he has built survives, he will receive a reward. ¹⁵ If anyone's work is burned up, he will experience loss, but he himself will be saved—but only as through fire.

¹⁶ Don't you yourselves know that you are God's temple and that the Spirit of God lives in you?

[17] If anyone destroys God's temple, God will destroy him; for God's temple is holy, and that is what you are.

THE FOLLY OF HUMAN WISDOM

[18] Let no one deceive himself. If anyone among you thinks he is wise in this age, let him become a fool so that he can become wise. [19] For the wisdom of this world is foolishness with God, since it is written, He catches the wise in their craftiness; [20] and again, The Lord knows that the reasonings of the wise are futile. [21] So let no one boast in human leaders, for everything is yours— [22] whether Paul or Apollos or Cephas or the world or life or death or things present or things to come—everything is yours, [23] and you belong to Christ, and Christ belongs to God.

♥ GOING DEEPER

Matthew 7:24–27

THE TWO FOUNDATIONS

[24] "Therefore, everyone who hears these words of mine and acts on them will be like a wise man who built his house on the rock. [25] The rain fell, the rivers rose, and the winds blew and pounded that house.

Yet it didn't collapse, because its foundation was on the rock.

[26] But everyone who hears these words of mine and doesn't act on them will be like a foolish man who built his house on the sand. [27] The rain fell, the rivers rose, the winds blew and pounded that house, and it collapsed. It collapsed with a great crash."

Romans 5:1

Therefore, since we have been justified by faith, we have peace with God through our Lord Jesus Christ.

Handwritten notes:

* division in the church leads to spiritual immaturity v. 1–4

* all spiritual growth is a work of the Lord and only He deserves glory and praise for it.

* the foundation of our faith is Jesus Christ.

* wisdom comes from Christ & Him alone.

An Example of Humility

1 Corinthians 4

THE FAITHFUL MANAGER

¹ A person should think of us in this way: as servants of Christ and managers of the mysteries of God. ² In this regard, it is required that managers be found faithful. ³ It is of little importance to me that I should be judged by you or by any human court. In fact, I don't even judge myself. ⁴ For I am not conscious of anything against myself, but I am not justified by this. It is the Lord who judges me. ⁵ So don't judge anything prematurely, before the Lord comes, who will both bring to light what is hidden in darkness and reveal the intentions of the hearts. And then praise will come to each one from God.

THE APOSTLES' EXAMPLE OF HUMILITY

⁶ Now, brothers and sisters, I have applied these things to myself and Apollos for your benefit, so that you may learn from us the meaning of the saying: "Nothing beyond what is written." The purpose is that none of you will be arrogant, favoring one person over another. ⁷ For who makes you so superior? What do you have that you didn't receive? If, in fact, you did receive it, why do you boast as if you hadn't received it? ⁸ You are already full! You are already rich! You have begun to reign as kings without us—and I wish you did reign, so that we could also reign with you! ⁹ For I think God has displayed us, the apostles, in last place, like men condemned to die: We have become a spectacle to the world, both to angels and to people. ¹⁰ We are fools for Christ, but you are wise in Christ! We are weak, but you are strong! You are distinguished, but we are dishonored! ¹¹ Up to the present hour we are both hungry and thirsty; we are poorly clothed, roughly treated, homeless; ¹² we labor, working with our own hands. When we are reviled, we bless; when we are persecuted, we endure it; ¹³ when we are slandered, we respond graciously. Even now, we are like the scum of the earth, like everyone's garbage.

PAUL'S FATHERLY CARE

¹⁴ I'm not writing this to shame you, but to warn you as my dear children. ¹⁵ For you may have

countless instructors in Christ, but you don't have many fathers. For I became your father in Christ Jesus through the gospel. [16] Therefore I urge you to imitate me. [17] This is why I have sent Timothy to you. He is my dearly loved and faithful child in the Lord. He will remind you about my ways in Christ Jesus, just as I teach everywhere in every church.

[18] Now some are arrogant, as though I were not coming to you. [19] But I will come to you soon, if the Lord wills, and I will find out not the talk, but the power of those who are arrogant. [20] For the kingdom of God is not a matter of talk but of power. [21] What do you want? Should I come to you with a rod, or in love and a spirit of gentleness?

♥ GOING DEEPER

Zephaniah 2:3
Seek the LORD, all you humble of the earth,
who carry out what he commands.
Seek righteousness, seek humility;
perhaps you will be concealed
on the day of the LORD's anger.

1 Peter 5:5
In the same way, you who are younger, be subject to the elders. All of you clothe yourselves with humility toward one another, because

God resists the proud
but gives grace to the humble.

* all we do should always point to God and His great work.

* Life in Christ is a life filled w/ hardship & suffering

* discipleship is a spiritual mothering sistering.

Church Discipline

1 Corinthians 5

IMMORAL CHURCH MEMBERS

[1] It is actually reported that there is sexual immorality among you, and the kind of sexual immorality that is not even tolerated among the Gentiles—a man is sleeping with his father's wife. [2] And you are arrogant! Shouldn't you be filled with grief and remove from your congregation the one who did this? [3] Even though I am absent in the body, I am present in spirit. As one who is present with you in this way, I have already pronounced judgment on the one who has been doing such a thing. [4] When you are assembled in the name of our Lord Jesus, and I am with you in spirit, with the power of our Lord Jesus, [5] hand that one over to Satan for the destruction of the flesh, so that his spirit may be saved in the day of the Lord.

[6] Your boasting is not good. Don't you know that a little leaven leavens the whole batch of dough? [7] Clean out the old leaven so that you may be a new unleavened batch, as indeed you are. For Christ our Passover lamb has been sacrificed. [8] Therefore, let us observe the feast, not with old leaven or with the leaven of malice and evil, but with the unleavened bread of sincerity and truth.

CHURCH DISCIPLINE

[9] I wrote to you in a letter not to associate with sexually immoral people. [10] I did not mean the immoral people of this world or the greedy and swindlers or idolaters; otherwise you would have to leave the world. [11] But actually, I wrote you not to associate with anyone who claims to be a brother or sister and is sexually immoral or greedy, an idolater or verbally abusive, a drunkard or a swindler. Do not even eat with such a person. [12] For what business is it of mine to judge outsiders? Don't you judge those who are inside? [13] God judges outsiders. Remove the evil person from among you.

Proverbs 15:31–33

31 One who listens to life-giving rebukes
will be at home among the wise.

32 Anyone who ignores discipline despises himself,
but whoever listens to correction acquires good sense.

33 The fear of the LORD is what wisdom teaches,
and humility comes before honor.

Galatians 6:1–10

CARRY ONE ANOTHER'S BURDENS

1 Brothers and sisters, if someone is overtaken in any wrongdoing,

you who are spiritual, restore such a person with a gentle spirit,

watching out for yourselves so that you also won't be tempted. 2 Carry one another's burdens; in this way you will fulfill the law of Christ. 3 For if anyone considers himself to be something when he is nothing, he deceives himself. 4 Let each person examine his own work, and then he can take pride in himself alone, and not compare himself with someone else. 5 For each person will have to carry his own load.

6 Let the one who is taught the word share all his good things with the teacher. 7 Don't be deceived: God is not mocked. For whatever a person sows he will also reap, 8 because the one who sows to his flesh will reap destruction from the flesh, but the one who sows to the Spirit will reap eternal life from the Spirit. 9 Let us not get tired of doing good, for we will reap at the proper time if we don't give up. 10 Therefore, as we have opportunity, let us work for the good of all, especially for those who belong to the household of faith.

* The Corinthian Church not only acted like the world, but so immoral even the world was disgusted.

* the case for ~~that~~ Church discipline is made here ↳ discipline should ~~always~~ have the goal of reconciliation!

* the judgement in v9–13 is less about condemning the sinner, but protecting the witness of the church to the world.

WEEKLY
RESPONSE

Week One

Look back through any notes you made this week as you answer the following questions.

1 What aspects of the Corinthian church surprised you?
What parts of their lives were confusing or different?

2 What teachings from this week's reading challenged you as a member of the body of Christ?

3 How would you like to practice those teachings in your own community this week?

① Not many aspects of the Corinthian church was surprising or confusing since I have studied this book before; both personally, in church, and in academic settings.

② All of the teaching are difficult when put into practice, living out humility & spiritual wisdom is easier said than done. Enacting church discipline is hard, its suppose to be! Living a holy life is never easy but it is a worthy and honorable endeavor!

③ I would like to practice <u>daily</u> reliance on the Holy Spirit's wisdom.

"He will also strengthen you to the end, so that you will be blameless in the day of our Lord Jesus Christ.
1 Corinthians 1:8

Grace

DAY 6

Day

Take this day to catch up on your
reading, pray, and rest in the
presence of the Lord.

Therefore, since we have
been justified by faith, we
have peace with God through
our Lord Jesus Christ.

ROMANS 5:1

Weekly Truth

Scripture is God-breathed and true. When we memorize it, we carry
the good news of Jesus with us wherever we go.

For the first part of this reading plan, we'll memorize 1 Corinthians 1:8–9,
the passage including our key verse for 1 Corinthians. We'll start with
verse 8, Paul's reminder of the source of our strength as we wait in hope
for Jesus to return, and work with Him to bring that hope to the world.

He will also strengthen you
to the end, so that you will
be blameless in the day of
our Lord Jesus Christ. God
is faithful; you were called by
him into fellowship with his
Son, Jesus Christ our Lord.

1 CORINTHIANS 1:8–9

See tips for memorizing Scripture on page 156.

Laci Fowler, *Flowers for Isla*, mixed media on canvas, 16x20 in.

Week Two

Glorifying God in Body and Spirit

1 Corinthians 6

LAWSUITS AMONG BELIEVERS

¹ If any of you has a dispute against another, how dare you take it to court before the unrighteous, and not before the saints? ² Or don't you know that the saints will judge the world? And if the world is judged by you, are you unworthy to judge the trivial cases? ³ Don't you know that we will judge angels—how much more matters of this life? ⁴ So if you have such matters, do you appoint as your judges those who have no standing in the church? ⁵ I say this to your shame! Can it be that there is not one wise person among you who is able to arbitrate between fellow believers? ⁶ Instead, brother goes to court against brother, and that before unbelievers!

⁷ As it is, to have legal disputes against one another is already a defeat for you. Why not rather be wronged? Why not rather be cheated? ⁸ Instead, you yourselves do wrong and cheat—and you do this to brothers and sisters! ⁹ Don't you know that the unrighteous will not inherit God's kingdom? Do not be deceived: No sexually immoral people,

idolaters, adulterers, or males who have sex with males, [10] no thieves, greedy people, drunkards, verbally abusive people, or swindlers will inherit God's kingdom. [11] And some of you used to be like this. But you were washed, you were sanctified, you were justified in the name of the Lord Jesus Christ and by the Spirit of our God.

GLORIFYING GOD IN BODY AND SPIRIT

[12] "Everything is permissible for me," but not everything is beneficial. "Everything is permissible for me," but I will not be mastered by anything. [13] "Food is for the stomach and the stomach for food," and God will do away with both of them. However, the body is not for sexual immorality but for the Lord, and the Lord for the body. [14] God raised up the Lord and will also raise us up by his power. [15] Don't you know that your bodies are a part of Christ's body? So should I take a part of Christ's body and make it part of a prostitute? Absolutely not! [16] Don't you know that anyone joined to a prostitute is one body with her? For Scripture says, The two will become one flesh.

[17] But anyone joined to the Lord is one spirit with him.

[18] Flee sexual immorality! Every other sin a person commits is outside the body, but the person who is sexually immoral sins against his own body. [19] Don't you know that your body is a temple of the Holy Spirit who is in you, whom you have from God? You are not your own, [20] for you were bought at a price. So glorify God with your body.

♥ GOING DEEPER

Leviticus 20:26

"You are to be holy to me because I, the LORD, am holy, and I have set you apart from the nations to be mine."

Titus 3:4–7

[4] But when the kindness of God our Savior and his love for mankind appeared, [5] he saved us—not by works of righteousness that we had done, but according to his mercy—through the washing of regeneration and renewal by the Holy Spirit. [6] He poured out his Spirit on us abundantly through Jesus Christ our Savior [7] so that, having been justified by his grace, we may become heirs with the hope of eternal life.

○ Christ should radically change our lives! I was once this way, but now I am as Christ.

our outward actions should (and do) reflect our inward realities

Spiritual → Physical

Principles of Marriage

1 Corinthians 7

PRINCIPLES OF MARRIAGE

¹ Now in response to the matters you wrote about: "It is good for a man not to have sexual relations with a woman." ² But because sexual immorality is so common, each man should have sexual relations with his own wife, and each woman should have sexual relations with her own husband. ³ A husband should fulfill his marital duty to his wife, and likewise a wife to her husband. ⁴ A wife does not have the right over her own body, but her husband does. In the same way, a husband does not have the right over his own body, but his wife does. ⁵ Do not deprive one another—except when you agree for a time, to devote yourselves to prayer. Then come together again; otherwise, Satan may tempt you because of your lack of self-control. ⁶ I say this as a concession, not as a command. ⁷ I wish that all people were as I am. But each has his own gift from God, one person has this gift, another has that.

the one flesh reality

A WORD TO THE UNMARRIED

⁸ I say to the unmarried and to widows: It is good for them if they remain as I am. ⁹ But if they do not have self-control, they should marry, since it is better to marry than to burn with desire.

ABOUT MARRIED PEOPLE

¹⁰ To the married I give this command—not I, but the Lord—a wife is not to leave her husband. ¹¹ But if she does leave, she must remain unmarried or be reconciled to her husband—and a husband is not to divorce his wife. ¹² But I (not the Lord) say to the rest: If any brother has an unbelieving wife and she is willing to live with him, he must not divorce her. ¹³ Also, if any woman has an unbelieving husband and he is willing to live with her, she must not divorce her husband. ¹⁴ For the unbelieving husband is made holy by the wife, and the unbelieving wife is made holy by the husband. Otherwise your children would be unclean, but as it is they are holy. ¹⁵ But if the unbeliever leaves, let him leave. A brother or a sister is not bound in such cases. God has called you to live in peace. ¹⁶ Wife, for all you know, you might save your husband. Husband, for all you know, you might save your wife.

CONTINUED

Let each one live his life in the situation the Lord assigned when God called him. This is what I command in all the churches.

1 CORINTHIANS 7:17

VARIOUS SITUATIONS OF LIFE

[17] Let each one live his life in the situation the Lord assigned when God called him. This is what I command in all the churches. [18] Was anyone already circumcised when he was called? He should not undo his circumcision. Was anyone called while uncircumcised? He should not get circumcised. [19] Circumcision does not matter and uncircumcision does not matter. Keeping God's commands is what matters. [20] Let each of you remain in the situation in which he was called. [21] Were you called while a slave? Don't let it concern you. But if you can become free, by all means take the opportunity. [22] For he who is called by the Lord as a slave is the Lord's freedman. Likewise he who is called as a free man is Christ's slave. [23] You were bought at a price; do not become slaves of people. [24] Brothers and sisters, each person is to remain with God in the situation in which he was called.

ABOUT THE UNMARRIED AND WIDOWS

[25] Now about virgins: I have no command from the Lord, but I do give an opinion as one who by the Lord's mercy is faithful. [26] Because of the present distress, I think that it is good for a man to remain as he is. [27] Are you bound to a wife? Do not seek to be released. Are you released from a wife? Do not seek a wife. [28] However, if you do get married, you have not sinned, and if a virgin marries, she has not sinned. But such people will have trouble in this life, and I am trying to spare you.

[29] This is what I mean, brothers and sisters: The time is limited, so from now on those who have wives should be as though they had none, [30] those who weep as though they did not weep, those who rejoice as though they did not rejoice, those who buy as though they didn't own anything, [31] and those who use the world as though they did not make full use of it. For this world in its current form is passing away. ✗ and will be made new!

[32] I want you to be without concerns. The unmarried man is concerned about the things of the Lord—how he may please the Lord. [33] But the married man is concerned about the things of the world—how he may please his wife— [34] and his interests are divided. The unmarried woman or virgin is concerned about the things of the Lord, so that she may be holy both in body and in spirit. But the married woman is concerned about the things of the world—how she may please her husband. [35] I am saying this for your own benefit, not to put a restraint on you, but to promote what is proper and so that you may be devoted to the Lord without distraction.

[36] If any man thinks he is acting improperly toward the virgin he is engaged to, if she is getting beyond the usual age for marriage, and he feels he should marry—he can do what he wants. He is not sinning; they can get married. [37] But he who stands firm in his heart (who is under no compulsion, but has control over his own

✗ marriage is a joyful trial that causes daily reminders of your sin.

will) and has decided in his heart to keep her as his fiancée, will do well. [38] So, then, he who marries his fiancée does well, but he who does not marry will do better.

[39] A wife is bound as long as her husband is living. But if her husband dies, she is free to be married to anyone she wants—only in the Lord. [40] But she is happier if she remains as she is, in my opinion. And I think that I also have the Spirit of God.

♥ GOING DEEPER

Genesis 2:24
This is why a man leaves his father and mother and bonds with his wife, and they become one flesh.

John 13:34–35
[34] "I give you a new command: Love one another. Just as I have loved you, you are also to love one another. [35] By this everyone will know that you are my disciples, if you love one another."

Food Offered to Idols

1 Corinthians 8
FOOD OFFERED TO IDOLS

¹ Now about food sacrificed to idols: We know that "we all have knowledge." Knowledge puffs up, but love builds up. ² If anyone thinks he knows anything, he does not yet know it as he ought to know it. ³ But if anyone loves God, he is known by him.

⁴ About eating food sacrificed to idols, then, we know that "an idol is nothing in the world," and that "there is no God but one." ⁵ For even if there are so-called gods, whether in heaven or on earth—as there are many "gods" and many "lords"— ⁶ yet for us there is one God, the Father. All things are from him, and we exist for him. And there is one Lord, Jesus Christ. All things are through him, and we exist through him.

⁷ However, not everyone has this knowledge. Some have been so used to idolatry up until now that when they eat food sacrificed to an idol, their conscience, being weak, is defiled. ⁸ Food will not bring us close to God. We are not worse off if we don't eat, and we are not better if we do eat. ⁹ But be careful that this right of yours in no way becomes a stumbling block to the weak. ¹⁰ For if someone sees you, the one who has knowledge, dining in an idol's temple, won't his weak conscience be encouraged to eat food offered to idols? ¹¹ So the weak person, the brother or sister for whom Christ died, is ruined by your knowledge. ¹² Now when you sin like this against brothers and sisters and wound their weak conscience, you are sinning against Christ. ¹³ Therefore, if food causes my brother or sister to fall, I will never again eat meat, so that I won't cause my brother or sister to fall.

🔖 GOING DEEPER

Romans 14:13–23
THE LAW OF LOVE

¹³ Therefore, let us no longer judge one another. Instead decide never to put a stumbling block or pitfall in the way of your brother or sister.

14 I know and am persuaded in the Lord Jesus that nothing is unclean in itself. Still, to someone who considers a thing to be unclean, to that one it is unclean. 15 For if your brother or sister is hurt by what you eat, you are no longer walking according to love. Do not destroy, by what you eat, someone for whom Christ died. 16 Therefore, do not let your good be slandered, 17 for the kingdom of God is not eating and drinking, but righteousness, peace, and joy in the Holy Spirit. 18 Whoever serves Christ in this way is acceptable to God and receives human approval.

19 So then, let us pursue what promotes peace and what builds up one another.

20 Do not tear down God's work because of food. Everything is clean, but it is wrong to make someone fall by what he eats. 21 It is a good thing not to eat meat, or drink wine, or do anything that makes your brother or sister stumble. 22 Whatever you believe about these things, keep between yourself and God. Blessed is the one who does not condemn himself by what he approves. 23 But whoever doubts stands condemned if he eats, because his eating is not from faith, and everything that is not from faith is sin.

Colossians 2:16–17

16 Therefore, don't let anyone judge you in regard to food and drink or in the matter of a festival or a new moon or a Sabbath day. 17 These are a shadow of what was to come; the substance is Christ.

Handwritten notes in margin:
- it not out offense to God that we avoid certain things – but out of love for our fellow brother

- it is also not my job to convince others of my personal convictions, but of the gospel.

Corinth in World History

776 BC
1. Ancient Olympic Games begin

550 BC
2. Temple of Apollo is constructed in Corinth

323 BC
3. Alexander the Great dies in Babylon

295 BC
4. Library in Alexandria is founded

146 BC
5. Corinth is destroyed by Rome

● Corinthian Events
● World Events

400   300   200   100   0   AD

51 BC

6 Cleopatra is named the coruler of Egypt

44 BC

7 Julius Caesar rebuilds Corinth as a colony of Rome

5 BC

8 Jesus is born

AD 33

9 Jesus dies, is resurrected, and ascends to heaven

AD 50/51

10 Claudius orders all Jews to leave Rome

Paul spends eighteen months in Corinth planting a church

Paul appears before Corinth's proconsul Gallio

AD 56

11 Paul writes 1 & 2 Corinthians

AD 57

12 Paul spends a few months in Corinth writing Romans

Paul's Example

1 Corinthians 9

PAUL'S EXAMPLE AS AN APOSTLE

1 Am I not free? Am I not an apostle? Have I not seen Jesus our Lord? Are you not my work in the Lord? 2 If I am not an apostle to others, at least I am to you, because you are the seal of my apostleship in the Lord.

3 My defense to those who examine me is this: 4 Don't we have the right to eat and drink? 5 Don't we have the right to be accompanied by a believing wife like the other apostles, the Lord's brothers, and Cephas? 6 Or do only Barnabas and I have no right to refrain from working? 7 Who serves as a soldier at his own expense? Who plants a vineyard and does not eat its fruit? Or who shepherds a flock and does not drink the milk from the flock?

8 Am I saying this from a human perspective? Doesn't the law also say the same thing? 9 For it is written in the law of Moses, Do not muzzle an ox while it treads out grain. Is God really concerned about oxen? 10 Isn't he really saying it for our sake? Yes, this is written for our sake, because he who plows ought to plow in hope, and he who threshes should thresh in hope of sharing the crop. 11 If we have sown spiritual things for you, is it too much if we reap material benefits from you? 12 If others have this right to receive benefits from you, don't we even more? Nevertheless, we have not made use of this right; instead, we endure everything so that we will not hinder the gospel of Christ.

13 Don't you know that those who perform the temple services eat the food from the temple, and those who serve at the altar share in the offerings of the altar? 14 In the same way, the Lord has commanded that those who preach the gospel should earn their living by the gospel.

15 For my part I have used none of these rights, nor have I written these things that they may be applied in my case. For it would be better for me to die than for anyone to deprive me of my boast! 16 For if I preach the gospel, I have no reason to boast, because I am compelled to preach—and

woe to me if I do not preach the gospel! [17] For if I do this willingly, I have a reward, but if unwillingly, I am entrusted with a commission. [18] What then is my reward? To preach the gospel and offer it free of charge and not make full use of my rights in the gospel.

[19] Although I am free from all and not anyone's slave, I have made myself a slave to everyone, in order to win more people. [20] To the Jews I became like a Jew, to win Jews; to those under the law, like one under the law—though I myself am not under the law—to win those under the law. [21] To those who are without the law, like one without the law—though I am not without God's law but under the law of Christ—to win those without the law. [22] To the weak I became weak, in order to win the weak. I have become all things to all people, so that I may by every possible means save some. [23] Now I do all this because of the gospel, so that I may share in the blessings.

[24] Don't you know that the runners in a stadium all race, but only one receives the prize? Run in such a way to win the prize. [25] Now everyone who competes exercises self-control in everything. They do it to receive a perishable crown, but we an imperishable crown. [26] So I do not run like one who runs aimlessly or box like one beating the air. [27] Instead, I discipline my body and bring it under strict control, so that after preaching to others, I myself will not be disqualified.

♥ GOING DEEPER

Romans 15:17–19

[17] Therefore I have reason to boast in Christ Jesus regarding what pertains to God. [18] For I would not dare say anything except what Christ has accomplished through me by word and deed for the obedience of the Gentiles, [19] by the power of miraculous signs and wonders, and by the power of God's Spirit. As a result, I have fully proclaimed the gospel of Christ from Jerusalem all the way around to Illyricum.

Hebrews 12:1–2

THE CALL TO ENDURANCE

[1] Therefore, since we also have such a large cloud of witnesses surrounding us, let us lay aside every hindrance and the sin that so easily ensnares us. Let us run with endurance the race that lies before us, [2] keeping our eyes on Jesus, the pioneer and perfecter of our faith. For the joy that lay before him, he endured the cross, despising the shame, and sat down at the right hand of the throne of God.

Warning from Israel's Past

1 Corinthians 10

WARNINGS FROM ISRAEL'S PAST

¹ Now I do not want you to be unaware, brothers and sisters, that our ancestors were all under the cloud, all passed through the sea, ² and all were baptized into Moses in the cloud and in the sea. ³ They all ate the same spiritual food, ⁴ and all drank the same spiritual drink. For they drank from the spiritual rock that followed them, and that rock was Christ. ⁵ Nevertheless God was not pleased with most of them, since they were struck down in the wilderness.

⁶ Now these things took place as examples for us, so that we will not desire evil things as they did. ⁷ Don't become idolaters as some of them were; as it is written, The people sat down to eat and drink, and got up to party. ⁸ Let us not commit sexual immorality as some of them did, and in a single day twenty-three thousand people died. ⁹ Let us not test Christ as some of them did and were destroyed by snakes. ¹⁰ And don't grumble as some of them did, and were killed by the destroyer.

¹¹ These things happened to them as examples, and they were written for our instruction, on whom the ends of the ages have come. ¹² So, whoever thinks he stands must be careful not to fall. ¹³ No temptation has come upon you except what is common to humanity. But God is faithful; he will not allow you to be tempted beyond what you are able, but with the temptation he will also provide the way out so that you may be able to bear it.

WARNING AGAINST IDOLATRY

¹⁴ So then, my dear friends, flee from idolatry. ¹⁵ I am speaking as to sensible people. Judge for yourselves what I am saying. ¹⁶ The cup of blessing that we bless, is it not a sharing in the blood of Christ? The bread that we break, is it not a sharing in the body of Christ? ¹⁷ Because there is one bread, we who are many are one body, since all of us share the one bread. ¹⁸ Consider the people of Israel. Do not those who eat the sacrifices participate in the altar? ¹⁹ What am I saying then?

CONTINUED

Now these things took place as examples for us, so that we will not desire evil things as they did.

1 CORINTHIANS 10:6

That food sacrificed to idols is anything, or that an idol is anything? ²⁰ No, but I do say that what they sacrifice, they sacrifice to demons and not to God. I do not want you to be participants with demons! ²¹ You cannot drink the cup of the Lord and the cup of demons. You cannot share in the Lord's table and the table of demons. ²² Or are we provoking the Lord to jealousy? Are we stronger than he?

CHRISTIAN LIBERTY

²³ "Everything is permissible," but not everything is beneficial. "Everything is permissible," but not everything builds up.

²⁴ No one is to seek his own good, but the good of the other person.

²⁵ Eat everything that is sold in the meat market, without raising questions for the sake of conscience, ²⁶ since the earth is the Lord's, and all that is in it. ²⁷ If any of the unbelievers invites you over and you want to go, eat everything that is set before you, without raising questions for the sake of conscience. ²⁸ But if someone says to you, "This is food from a sacrifice," do not eat it, out of consideration for the one who told you, and for the sake of conscience. ²⁹ I do not mean your own conscience, but the other person's. For why is my freedom judged by another person's conscience? ³⁰ If I partake with thanksgiving, why am I criticized because of something for which I give thanks?

³¹ So, whether you eat or drink, or whatever you do, do everything for the glory of God. ³² Give no offense to Jews or Greeks or the church of God, ³³ just as I also try to please everyone in everything, not seeking my own benefit, but the benefit of many, so that they may be saved.

1 Corinthians 11:1
Imitate me, as I also imitate Christ.

🍂 GOING DEEPER

Exodus 13:17–22
THE ROUTE OF THE EXODUS

¹⁷ When Pharaoh let the people go, God did not lead them along the road to the land of the Philistines, even though it was nearby; for God said, "The people will change their minds and return to Egypt if they face war." ¹⁸ So he led the people around toward the Red Sea along the road of the wilderness. And the Israelites left the land of Egypt in battle formation.

¹⁹ Moses took the bones of Joseph with him, because Joseph had made the Israelites swear a solemn oath, saying, "God will certainly come to your aid; then you must take my bones with you from this place."

²⁰ They set out from Succoth and camped at Etham on the edge of the wilderness. ²¹ The Lᴏʀᴅ went ahead of them in a pillar of cloud to lead them on their way during the day and in a pillar of fire to give them light at night, so that they could travel day or night. ²² The pillar of cloud by day and the pillar of fire by night never left its place in front of the people.

Hebrews 3:7–19
WARNING AGAINST UNBELIEF

⁷ Therefore, as the Holy Spirit says:

Today, if you hear his voice,
⁸ do not harden your hearts as in the rebellion,
on the day of testing in the wilderness,
⁹ where your ancestors tested me, tried me,
and saw my works ¹⁰ for forty years.
Therefore I was provoked to anger with that generation
and said, "They always go astray in their hearts,
and they have not known my ways."
¹¹ So I swore in my anger,
"They will not enter my rest."

¹² Watch out, brothers and sisters, so that there won't be in any of you an evil, unbelieving heart that turns away from the living God. ¹³ But encourage each other daily, while it is still called today, so that none of you is hardened by sin's deception. ¹⁴ For we have become participants in Christ if we hold firmly until the end the reality that we had at the start. ¹⁵ As it is said:

Today, if you hear his voice,
do not harden your hearts as in the rebellion.

¹⁶ For who heard and rebelled? Wasn't it all who came out of Egypt under Moses? ¹⁷ With whom was God angry for forty years? Wasn't it with those who sinned, whose bodies fell in the wilderness? ¹⁸ And to whom did he swear that they would not enter his rest, if not to those who disobeyed? ¹⁹ So we see that they were unable to enter because of unbelief.

SHE READS TRUTH   DAY 12   57

Week Two

Look back through any notes you made this week as you answer the following questions.

1 What aspects of the Corinthian church surprised you?
What parts of their lives were confusing or different?

2 What teachings from this week's reading challenged you as a member of the body of Christ?

3 How would you like to practice those teachings in your own community this week?

- He will also strengthen you to the end, so that you will be blameless in the day of our Lord Jesus Christ. 1 Corinthians 1:8
- He will also strengthen you to the end, so that you will be blameless in the day of our Lord Jesus Christ 1 Corinthians 1:8
- He will also strengthen you to the end, so that you will be blameless in the day of our Lord Jesus Christ - 1 Corinthians 1:8
- He will also strengthen you to the end, so that you will be blameless in the day of our Lord Jesus Christ - 1 Corinthians 1:8

Grace

DAY 13

Day

Take this day to catch up on your
reading, pray, and rest in the
presence of the Lord.

"You are to be holy to me
because I, the LORD, am
holy, and I have set you
apart from the nations
to be mine."

LEVITICUS 20:26

DAY 14

Weekly Truth

Scripture is God-breathed and true. When we memorize it,
we carry the good news of Jesus with us wherever we go.

For the first half of this plan, we are memorizing 1 Corinthians 1:8–9.
This week we will memorize verse 9, the declaration of our identity
in Christ because of God's faithfulness.

He will also strengthen you to the end, so that you will be blameless in the day of our Lord Jesus Christ. **God is faithful; you were called by him into fellowship with his Son, Jesus Christ our Lord.**

1 CORINTHIANS 1:8–9

See tips for memorizing Scripture on page 156.

Laci Fowler, *Spring Morning*, mixed media on canvas, 11x14 in.

Week Three

The Lord's Supper

1 Corinthians 11:2–34
INSTRUCTIONS ABOUT HEAD COVERINGS

[2] Now I praise you because you remember me in everything and hold fast to the traditions just as I delivered them to you. [3] But I want you to know that Christ is the head of every man, and the man is the head of the woman, and God is the head of Christ. [4] Every man who prays or prophesies with something on his head dishonors his head. [5] Every woman who prays or prophesies with her head uncovered dishonors her head, since that is one and the same as having her head shaved. [6] For if a woman doesn't cover her head, she should have her hair cut off. But if it is disgraceful for a woman to have her hair cut off or her head shaved, let her head be covered.

[7] A man should not cover his head, because he is the image and glory of God. So too, woman is the glory of man. [8] For man did not come from woman, but woman came from man. [9] Neither was man created for the sake of woman, but woman for the sake of man. [10] This is why a woman should

have a symbol of authority on her head, because of the angels. [11] In the Lord, however, woman is not independent of man, and man is not independent of woman. [12] For just as woman came from man, so man comes through woman, and all things come from God.

[13] Judge for yourselves: Is it proper for a woman to pray to God with her head uncovered? [14] Does not even nature itself teach you that if a man has long hair it is a disgrace to him, [15] but that if a woman has long hair, it is her glory? For her hair is given to her as a covering. [16] If anyone wants to argue about this, we have no other custom, nor do the churches of God.

THE LORD'S SUPPER

[17] Now in giving this instruction I do not praise you, since you come together not for the better but for the worse. [18] For to begin with, I hear that when you come together as a church there are divisions among you, and in part I believe it. [19] Indeed, it is necessary that there be factions among you, so that those who are approved may be recognized among you. [20] When you come together, then, it is not to eat the Lord's Supper. [21] For at the meal, each one eats his own supper. So one person is hungry while another gets drunk! [22] Don't you have homes in which to eat and drink? Or do you despise the church of God and humiliate those who have nothing? What should I say to you? Should I praise you? I do not praise you in this matter!

[23] For I received from the Lord what I also passed on to you: On the night when he was betrayed, the Lord Jesus took bread, [24] and when he had given thanks, broke it, and said,

"This is my body, which is for you. Do this in remembrance of me."

[25] In the same way also he took the cup, after supper, and said, "This cup is the new covenant in my blood. Do this, as often as you drink it, in remembrance of me." [26] For as often as you eat this bread and drink the cup, you proclaim the Lord's death until he comes.

SELF-EXAMINATION

[27] So, then, whoever eats the bread or drinks the cup of the Lord in an unworthy manner will be guilty of sin against the body and blood of the Lord. [28] Let a person examine himself; in this way let him eat the bread and drink from the cup. [29] For whoever eats and drinks without recognizing the body, eats and drinks judgment on himself. [30] This is why many are sick and ill among you, and many have fallen asleep. [31] If we were properly judging ourselves, we would not be judged,

[32] but when we are judged by the Lord, we are disciplined, so that we may not be condemned with the world.

[33] Therefore, my brothers and sisters, when you come together to eat, welcome one another. [34] If anyone is hungry, he should eat at home, so that when you gather together you will not come under judgment. I will give instructions about the other matters whenever I come.

GOING DEEPER

Matthew 26:26–28

THE FIRST LORD'S SUPPER

[26] As they were eating, Jesus took bread, blessed and broke it, gave it to the disciples, and said, "Take and eat it; this is my body." [27] Then he took a cup, and after giving thanks, he gave it to them and said, "Drink from it, all of you. [28] For this is my blood of the covenant, which is poured out for many for the forgiveness of sins."

Romans 3:25–26

[25] God presented him as the mercy seat by his blood, through faith, to demonstrate his righteousness, because in his restraint God passed over the sins previously committed. [26] God presented him to demonstrate his righteousness at the present time, so that he would be just and justify the one who has faith in Jesus.

The Lord's Supper

The Lord's Supper was established by Jesus when He observed the Passover meal with His disciples. When we participate in it, we proclaim the gospel to ourselves and to one another. Though denominations differ in frequency and manner of practice, this overview offers a look at what Scripture teaches us about the Lord's Supper.

Known As

THE LORD'S SUPPER
1Co 11:20

COMMUNION
1Co 10:16

THE EUCHARIST
1Co 11:24

Origin

ESTABLISHED BY JESUS
Jesus took bread, blessed and broke it.
Mt 26:26

**INTRODUCED DURING
A PASSOVER CELEBRATION**
They prepared the Passover.
Mk 14:16

**FIRST TOOK PLACE
DURING HOLY WEEK**
On the night when he was betrayed…
1Co 11:23

SHARED WITH JESUS'S DISCIPLES
He took bread…gave it to them…
Lk 22:19

**CONSISTED OF UNLEAVENED
BREAD AND WINE**
He took bread….then he took a cup…
Mk 14:22–23

Practice

PREPARE WITH SELF-EXAMINATION

Let a person examine himself; in this way let him eat the bread and drink from the cup.

1Co 11:28

APPROACH THE LORD'S
SUPPER WITH REVERENCE

Whoever eats the bread or drinks the cup of the Lord in an unworthy manner will be guilty of sin against the body and blood of the Lord.

1Co 11:27

Purpose

TO REMEMBER CHRIST'S SACRIFICE

"This is my body, which is given for you. Do this in remembrance of me."

Lk 22:19

FOR JESUS TO PRESENT HIMSELF
AS THE PERFECT PASSOVER LAMB

"This cup is the new covenant in my blood, which is poured out for you."

Lk 22:20

FOR THE CHURCH TO PROCLAIM
THE PERSON AND WORK OF CHRIST

You proclaim the Lord's death until he comes.

1Co 11:26

Unity and Diversity in the Body

1 Corinthians 12

DIVERSITY OF SPIRITUAL GIFTS

¹ Now concerning spiritual gifts: brothers and sisters, I do not want you to be unaware. ² You know that when you were pagans, you used to be enticed and led astray by mute idols. ³ Therefore I want you to know that no one speaking by the Spirit of God says, "Jesus is cursed," and no one can say, "Jesus is Lord," except by the Holy Spirit.

⁴ Now there are different gifts, but the same Spirit. ⁵ There are different ministries, but the same Lord. ⁶ And there are different activities, but the same God works all of them in each person. ⁷ A manifestation of the Spirit is given to each person for the common good: ⁸ to one is given a message of wisdom through the Spirit, to another, a message of knowledge by the same Spirit, ⁹ to another, faith by the same Spirit, to another, gifts of healing by the one Spirit, ¹⁰ to another, the performing of miracles, to another, prophecy, to another, distinguishing between spirits, to another, different kinds of tongues, to another, interpretation of tongues. ¹¹ One and the same Spirit is active in all these, distributing to each person as he wills.

UNITY YET DIVERSITY IN THE BODY

¹² For just as the body is one and has many parts, and all the parts of that body, though many, are one body—so also is Christ. ¹³ For we were all baptized by one Spirit into one body—whether Jews or Greeks, whether slaves or free—and we were all given one Spirit to drink. ¹⁴ Indeed, the body is not one part but many. ¹⁵ If the foot should say, "Because I'm not a hand, I don't belong to the body," it is not for that reason any less a part of the body. ¹⁶ And if the ear should say, "Because I'm not an eye, I don't belong to the body," it is not for that reason any less a part of the body. ¹⁷ If the whole body were an eye, where would the hearing be? If the whole body were an ear, where would the sense of smell be? ¹⁸ But as it is, God has arranged each one of the parts in the body just as he wanted. ¹⁹ And if they were all the same part, where would the body be? ²⁰ As it is,

there are many parts, but one body. [21] The eye cannot say to the hand, "I don't need you!" Or again, the head can't say to the feet, "I don't need you!" [22] On the contrary, those parts of the body that are weaker are indispensable. [23] And those parts of the body that we consider less honorable, we clothe these with greater honor, and our unrespectable parts are treated with greater respect, [24] which our respectable parts do not need.

Instead, God has put the body together,

giving greater honor to the less honorable, [25] so that there would be no division in the body, but that the members would have the same concern for each other. [26] So if one member suffers, all the members suffer with it; if one member is honored, all the members rejoice with it.

[27] Now you are the body of Christ, and individual members of it. [28] And God has appointed these in the church: first apostles, second prophets, third teachers, next miracles, then gifts of healing, helping, leading, various kinds of tongues. [29] Are all apostles? Are all prophets? Are all teachers? Do all do miracles? [30] Do all have gifts of healing? Do all speak in tongues? Do all interpret? [31] But desire the greater gifts. And I will show you an even better way.

◆ GOING DEEPER

Romans 12:4–5

[4] Now as we have many parts in one body, and all the parts do not have the same function, [5] in the same way we who are many are one body in Christ and individually members of one another.

1 Thessalonians 5:19–21

[19] Don't stifle the Spirit. [20] Don't despise prophecies, [21] but test all things. Hold on to what is good.

Love, the Superior Way

1 Corinthians 13

LOVE: THE SUPERIOR WAY

[1] If I speak human or angelic tongues but do not have love, I am a noisy gong or a clanging cymbal. [2] If I have the gift of prophecy and understand all mysteries and all knowledge, and if I have all faith so that I can move mountains but do not have love, I am nothing. [3] And if I give away all my possessions, and if I give over my body in order to boast but do not have love, I gain nothing.

[4] Love is patient, love is kind. Love does not envy, is not boastful, is not arrogant, [5] is not rude, is not self-seeking, is not irritable, and does not keep a record of wrongs. [6] Love finds no joy in unrighteousness but rejoices in the truth. [7] It bears all things, believes all things, hopes all things, endures all things.

[8] Love never ends. But as for prophecies, they will come to an end; as for tongues, they will cease; as for knowledge, it will come to an end. [9] For we know in part, and we prophesy in part, [10] but when the perfect comes, the partial will come to an end. [11] When I was a child, I spoke like a child, I thought like a child, I reasoned like a child. When I became a man, I put aside childish things. [12] For now we see only a reflection as in a mirror, but then face to face. Now I know in part, but then I will know fully, as I am fully known. [13] Now these three remain: faith, hope, and love—but the greatest of these is love.

🐚 GOING DEEPER

Psalm 145:8–10, 14–19

[8] The LORD is gracious and compassionate,
slow to anger and great in faithful love.
[9] The LORD is good to everyone;
his compassion rests on all he has made.
[10] All you have made will thank you, LORD;
the faithful will bless you.
…

¹⁴ The LORD helps all who fall;

he raises up all who are oppressed.

¹⁵ All eyes look to you,

and you give them their food at the proper time.

¹⁶ You open your hand

and satisfy the desire of every living thing.

¹⁷ The LORD is righteous in all his ways

and faithful in all his acts.

¹⁸ The LORD is near all who call out to him,

all who call out to him with integrity.

¹⁹ He fulfills the desires of those who fear him;

he hears their cry for help and saves them.

John 15:9–17

CHRISTLIKE LOVE

⁹ "As the Father has loved me, I have also loved you.

Remain in my love.

¹⁰ If you keep my commands you will remain in my love, just as I have kept my Father's commands and remain in his love.

¹¹ "I have told you these things so that my joy may be in you and your joy may be complete.

¹² "This is my command: Love one another as I have loved you. ¹³ No one has greater love than this: to lay down his life for his friends. ¹⁴ You are my friends if you do what I command you. ¹⁵ I do not call you servants anymore, because a servant doesn't know what his master is doing. I have called you friends, because I have made known to you everything I have heard from my Father. ¹⁶ You did not choose me, but I chose you. I appointed you to go and produce fruit and that your fruit should remain, so that whatever you ask the Father in my name, he will give you.

¹⁷ "This is what I command you: Love one another."

Gifts from the Holy Spirit

1 Corinthians 14

PROPHECY: A SUPERIOR GIFT

[1] Pursue love and desire spiritual gifts, and especially that you may prophesy. [2] For the person who speaks in a tongue is not speaking to people but to God, since no one understands him; he speaks mysteries in the Spirit. [3] On the other hand, the person who prophesies speaks to people for their strengthening, encouragement, and consolation. [4] The person who speaks in a tongue builds himself up, but the one who prophesies builds up the church. [5] I wish all of you spoke in tongues, but even more that you prophesied. The person who prophesies is greater than the person who speaks in tongues, unless he interprets so that the church may be built up.

[6] So now, brothers and sisters, if I come to you speaking in tongues, how will I benefit you unless I speak to you with a revelation or knowledge or prophecy or teaching? [7] Even lifeless instruments that produce sounds—whether flute or harp—if they don't make a distinction in the notes, how will what is played on the flute or harp be recognized? [8] In fact, if the bugle makes an unclear sound, who will prepare for battle? [9] In the same way, unless you use your tongue for intelligible speech, how will what is spoken be known? For you will be speaking into the air. [10] There are doubtless many different kinds of languages in the world, none is without meaning. [11] Therefore, if I do not know the meaning of the language, I will be a foreigner to the speaker, and the speaker will be a foreigner to me. [12] So also you—since you are zealous for spiritual gifts, seek to excel in building up the church.

[13] Therefore the person who speaks in a tongue should pray that he can interpret. [14] For if I pray in a tongue, my spirit prays, but my understanding is unfruitful. [15] What then? I will pray with the spirit, and I will also pray with my understanding. I will sing praise with the spirit, and I will also sing praise with my understanding. [16] Otherwise, if you praise with the spirit, how will the outsider say "Amen" at your giving of thanks, since he does not know what you are saying? [17] For you may very well be giving thanks, but the other person is not being built up. [18] I thank God that I speak in tongues more than all of you; [19] yet in the church I would rather speak five words with my understanding, in order to teach others also, than ten thousand words in a tongue.

[20] Brothers and sisters, don't be childish in your thinking, but be infants in regard to evil and adult in your thinking. [21] It is written in the law,

CONTINUED

…seek to excel in building up the church.

1 CORINTHIANS 14:12

I will speak to this people
by people of other tongues
and by the lips of foreigners,
and even then, they will not listen to me,

says the Lord. ²² Speaking in tongues, then, is intended as a sign, not for believers but for unbelievers, while prophecy is not for unbelievers but for believers. ²³ If, therefore, the whole church assembles together and all are speaking in tongues and people who are outsiders or unbelievers come in, will they not say that you are out of your minds? ²⁴ But if all are prophesying and some unbeliever or outsider comes in, he is convicted by all and is called to account by all. ²⁵ The secrets of his heart will be revealed, and as a result he will fall facedown and worship God, proclaiming, "God is really among you."

ORDER IN CHURCH MEETINGS

²⁶ What then, brothers and sisters? Whenever you come together, each one has a hymn, a teaching, a revelation, a tongue, or an interpretation. Everything is to be done for building up. ²⁷ If anyone speaks in a tongue, there are to be only two, or at the most three, each in turn, and let someone interpret. ²⁸ But if there is no interpreter, that person is to keep silent in the church and speak to himself and God. ²⁹ Two or three prophets should speak, and the others should evaluate. ³⁰ But if something has been revealed to another person sitting there, the first prophet should be silent. ³¹ For you can all prophesy one by one, so that everyone may learn and everyone may be encouraged. ³² And the prophets' spirits are subject to the prophets, ³³ since God is not a God of disorder but of peace.

As in all the churches of the saints, ³⁴ the women should be silent in the churches, for they are not permitted to speak, but are to submit themselves, as the law also says. ³⁵ If they want to learn something, let them ask their own husbands at home, since it is disgraceful for a woman to speak in the church. ³⁶ Or did the word of God originate from you, or did it come to you only?

³⁷ If anyone thinks he is a prophet or spiritual, he should recognize that what I write to you is the Lord's command.

³⁸ If anyone ignores this, he will be ignored. ³⁹ So then, my brothers and sisters, be eager to prophesy, and do not forbid speaking in tongues. ⁴⁰ But everything is to be done decently and in order.

◖ GOING DEEPER

Joel 2:28–32
GOD'S PROMISE OF HIS SPIRIT

²⁸ "After this
I will pour out my Spirit on all humanity;
then your sons and your daughters will prophesy,
your old men will have dreams,
and your young men will see visions.
²⁹ I will even pour out my Spirit
on the male and female slaves in those days.
³⁰ I will display wonders
in the heavens and on the earth:
blood, fire, and columns of smoke.
³¹ The sun will be turned to darkness
and the moon to blood
before the great and terrible day of the LORD comes.
³² Then everyone who calls
on the name of the LORD will be saved,
for there will be an escape
for those on Mount Zion and in Jerusalem,
as the LORD promised,
among the survivors the LORD calls."

1 John 4:1–3
THE SPIRIT OF TRUTH AND THE SPIRIT OF ERROR

¹ Dear friends, do not believe every spirit, but test the spirits to see if they are from God, because many false prophets have gone out into the world.

² This is how you know the Spirit of God: Every spirit that confesses that Jesus Christ has come in the flesh is from God, ³ but every spirit that does not confess Jesus is not from God. This is the spirit of the antichrist, which you have heard is coming; even now it is already in the world.

Spiritual Gifts

ESSENTIAL GIFTS

- PRESENCE OF THE HOLY SPIRIT Ac 2:1–4, 15–18
- LOVE Rm 5:5
- HOPE Rm 8:23–25
- FAITH 1Co 12:8–10; Eph 2:8–9

DYNAMIC GIFTS

- PROPHECY Rm 12:6–8; 1Co 12:8–10
- DISCERNMENT OF SPIRITS 1Co 12:8–10
- HEALING 1Co 12:8–10, 28–30
- MIRACLES 1Co 12:8–10, 28–30
- TONGUES 1Co 12:8–10, 28–30
- INTERPRETATION OF TONGUES 1Co 12:8–10, 28–30

FUNCTIONAL GIFTS

ABILITIES

- HELPING 1Co 12:28
- EXHORTATION Rm 12:6–8
- GENEROSITY Rm 12:6–8
- HOSPITALITY 1Pt 4:9
- KNOWLEDGE 1Co 12:8–10
- MERCY Rm 12:6–8
- SERVICE Rm 12:6–8; 1Pt 4:10–11
- WISDOM 1Co 12:8–10

ROLES

- TEACHER Rm 12:6–8; 1Co 12:28–30; Eph 4:11
- LEADER Rm 12:6–8
- PROPHET 1Co 12:28–30; Eph 4:11
- PASTOR Eph 4:11
- EVANGELIST Eph 4:11
- APOSTLE 1Co 12:28–30; Eph 4:11

Spiritual gifts are one way God equips the Church for the life and work He calls us to. These gifts range from essentials for the Christian life to miraculous abilities to roles and skills necessary for the ongoing ministry of the Church. While the gifts on this list vary in type, they all share one distinctive quality: they come directly from the Holy Spirit.

Essential Gifts

Qualities given to all believers everywhere that are necessary for living the Christian life

Dynamic Gifts

Special abilities given for the distinct purpose of delivering or validating a message from God

Functional Gifts

Roles and abilities needed for the ongoing structure and ministry of the Church

Some Christian traditions believe that dynamic gifts ceased early in Church history. Others hold they still are accessible today.

Essential Resurrection

1 Corinthians 15:1–19

RESURRECTION ESSENTIAL TO THE GOSPEL

[1] Now I want to make clear for you, brothers and sisters, the gospel I preached to you, which you received, on which you have taken your stand [2] and by which you are being saved, if you hold to the message I preached to you—unless you believed in vain. [3] For I passed on to you as most important what I also received: that Christ died for our sins according to the Scriptures, [4] that he was buried, that he was raised on the third day according to the Scriptures, [5] and that he appeared to Cephas, then to the Twelve. [6] Then he appeared to over five hundred brothers and sisters at one time; most of them are still alive, but some have fallen asleep. [7] Then he appeared to James, then to all the apostles. [8] Last of all, as to one born at the wrong time, he also appeared to me.

[9] For I am the least of the apostles, not worthy to be called an apostle, because I persecuted the church of God. [10] But by the grace of God I am what I am, and his grace toward me was not in vain. On the contrary, I worked harder than any of them, yet not I, but the grace of God that was with me. [11] Whether, then, it is I or they,

so we proclaim and so you have believed.

RESURRECTION ESSENTIAL TO THE FAITH

[12] Now if Christ is proclaimed as raised from the dead, how can some of you say, "There is no resurrection of the dead"? [13] If there is no resurrection of the dead, then not even Christ has been raised; [14] and if Christ has not been raised, then our proclamation is in vain, and so is your faith. [15] Moreover, we are found to be false witnesses about God, because we have testified wrongly about God that he raised up Christ—whom he did not raise up, if in fact the dead are not raised. [16] For if the dead are not raised, not even Christ has been raised. [17] And if Christ has not been raised, your faith is worthless; you are still in your sins. [18] Those, then, who have

fallen asleep in Christ have also perished. [19] If we have put our hope in Christ for this life only, we should be pitied more than anyone.

❤ GOING DEEPER

Ephesians 2:4–7

[4] But God, who is rich in mercy, because of his great love that he had for us, [5] made us alive with Christ even though we were dead in trespasses. You are saved by grace! [6] He also raised us up with him and seated us with him in the heavens in Christ Jesus, [7] so that in the coming ages he might display the immeasurable riches of his grace through his kindness to us in Christ Jesus.

Hebrews 2:5–9

JESUS AND HUMANITY

[5] For he has not subjected to angels the world to come that we are talking about. [6] But someone somewhere has testified:

What is man that you remember him,
or the son of man that you care for him?
[7] You made him lower than the angels
for a short time;
you crowned him with glory and honor
[8] and subjected everything under his feet.

For in subjecting everything to him, he left nothing that is not subject to him. As it is, we do not yet see everything subjected to him. [9] But we do see Jesus—made lower than the angels for a short time so that by God's grace he might taste death for everyone—crowned with glory and honor because he suffered death.

Week Three

Look back through any notes you made this week as you answer the following questions.

1 What aspects of the Corinthian church surprised you?
What parts of their lives were confusing or different?

2 What teachings from this week's reading challenged you as a member of the body of Christ?

3 How would you like to practice those teachings in your own community this week?

NOTES

Grace

DAY 20

Day

Take this day to catch up on your
reading, pray, and rest in the
presence of the Lord.

"As the Father has loved
me, I have also loved you.
Remain in my love."

JOHN 15:9

Weekly Truth

Scripture is God-breathed and true. When we memorize it,
we carry the good news of Jesus with us wherever we go.

For the last two weeks, we've memorized 1 Corinthians 1:8–9.
Now, let's put the entire passage together.

He will also strengthen you
to the end, so that you will
be blameless in the day of
our Lord Jesus Christ. God
is faithful; you were called by
him into fellowship with his
Son, Jesus Christ our Lord.

1 CORINTHIANS 1:8–9

See tips for memorizing Scripture on page 156.

Laci Fowler, *Fruity*, mixed media on canvas, 22x28 in.

Week Four

Victorious Resurrection

1 Corinthians 15:20–58
CHRIST'S RESURRECTION GUARANTEES OURS

20 But as it is, Christ has been raised from the dead, the firstfruits of those who have fallen asleep. 21 For since death came through a man, the resurrection of the dead also comes through a man. 22 For just as in Adam all die, so also in Christ all will be made alive.

23 But each in his own order: Christ, the firstfruits; afterward, at his coming, those who belong to Christ. 24 Then comes the end, when he hands over the kingdom to God the Father, when he abolishes all rule and all authority and power. 25 For he must reign until he puts all his enemies under his feet. 26 The last enemy to be abolished is death. 27 For God has put everything under his feet. Now when it says "everything" is put under him, it is obvious that he who puts everything under him is the exception. 28 When everything is subject to Christ, then the Son himself will also be subject to the one who subjected everything to him, so that God may be all in all.

RESURRECTION SUPPORTED BY CHRISTIAN EXPERIENCE

[29] Otherwise what will they do who are being baptized for the dead? If the dead are not raised at all, then why are people baptized for them? [30] Why are we in danger every hour? [31] I face death every day, as surely as I may boast about you, brothers and sisters, in Christ Jesus our Lord. [32] If I fought wild beasts in Ephesus as a mere man, what good did that do me? If the dead are not raised, Let us eat and drink, for tomorrow we die. [33] Do not be deceived: "Bad company corrupts good morals." [34] Come to your senses and stop sinning; for some people are ignorant about God. I say this to your shame.

THE NATURE OF THE RESURRECTION BODY

[35] But someone will ask, "How are the dead raised? What kind of body will they have when they come?" [36] You fool! What you sow does not come to life unless it dies. [37] And as for what you sow—you are not sowing the body that will be, but only a seed, perhaps of wheat or another grain. [38] But God gives it a body as he wants, and to each of the seeds its own body. [39] Not all flesh is the same flesh; there is one flesh for humans, another for animals, another for birds, and another for fish. [40] There are heavenly bodies and earthly bodies, but the splendor of the heavenly bodies is different from that of the earthly ones. [41] There is a splendor of the sun, another of the moon, and another of the stars; in fact, one star differs from another star in splendor. [42] So it is with the resurrection of the dead: Sown in corruption, raised in incorruption; [43] sown in dishonor, raised in glory; sown in weakness, raised in power; [44] sown a natural body, raised a spiritual body. If there is a natural body, there is also a spiritual body. [45] So it is written, The first man Adam became a living being; the last Adam became a life-giving spirit. [46] However, the spiritual is not first, but the natural, then the spiritual.

[47] The first man was from the earth, a man of dust; the second man is from heaven. [48] Like the man of dust, so are those who are of the dust; like the man of heaven, so are those who are of heaven. [49] And just as we have borne the image of the man of dust, we will also bear the image of the man of heaven.

VICTORIOUS RESURRECTION

[50] What I am saying, brothers and sisters, is this: Flesh and blood cannot inherit the kingdom of God, nor can corruption inherit incorruption. [51] Listen, I am telling you a mystery: We will not all fall asleep, but we will all be changed, [52] in

a moment, in the twinkling of an eye, at the last trumpet. For the trumpet will sound, and the dead will be raised incorruptible, and we will be changed. ⁵³ For this corruptible body must be clothed with incorruptibility, and this mortal body must be clothed with immortality. ⁵⁴ When this corruptible body is clothed with incorruptibility, and this mortal body is clothed with immortality, then the saying that is written will take place:

Death has been swallowed up in victory.
⁵⁵ Where, death, is your victory?
Where, death, is your sting?

⁵⁶ The sting of death is sin, and the power of sin is the law. ⁵⁷ But thanks be to God, who gives us the victory through our Lord Jesus Christ!

⁵⁸ Therefore, my dear brothers and sisters, be steadfast, immovable, always excelling in the Lord's work, because you know that your labor in the Lord is not in vain.

♥ GOING DEEPER

Romans 6:3–11

³ Or are you unaware that all of us who were baptized into Christ Jesus were baptized into his death? ⁴ Therefore we were buried with him by baptism into death, in order that, just as Christ was raised from the dead by the glory of the Father, so we too may walk in newness of life. ⁵ For if we have been united with him in the likeness of his death, we will certainly also be in the likeness of his resurrection. ⁶ For we know that our old self was crucified with him so that the body ruled by sin might be rendered powerless so that we may no longer be enslaved to sin, ⁷ since a person who has died is freed from sin. ⁸ Now if we died with Christ, we believe that we will also live with him, ⁹ because we know that Christ, having been raised from the dead, will not die again. Death no longer rules over him. ¹⁰ For the death he died, he died to sin once for all time; but the life he lives, he lives to God. ¹¹ So, you too consider yourselves dead to sin and alive to God in Christ Jesus.

Philippians 1:21

For me, to live is Christ and to die is gain.

The Lord's Work

1 Corinthians 16

COLLECTION FOR THE JERUSALEM CHURCH

¹ Now about the collection for the saints: Do the same as I instructed the Galatian churches. ² On the first day of the week, each of you is to set something aside and save in keeping with how he is prospering, so that no collections will need to be made when I come. ³ When I arrive, I will send with letters those you recommend to carry your gift to Jerusalem. ⁴ If it is suitable for me to go as well, they will travel with me.

PAUL'S TRAVEL PLANS

⁵ I will come to you after I pass through Macedonia—for I will be traveling through Macedonia— ⁶ and perhaps I will remain with you or even spend the winter, so that you may send me on my way wherever I go. ⁷ I don't want to see you now just in passing, since I hope to spend some time with you, if the Lord allows. ⁸ But I will stay in Ephesus until Pentecost, ⁹ because a wide door for effective ministry has opened for me—yet many oppose me. ¹⁰ If Timothy comes, see that

he has nothing to fear while with you, because he is doing the Lord's work, just as I am. ¹¹ So let no one look down on him. Send him on his way in peace so that he can come to me, because I am expecting him with the brothers.

¹² Now about our brother Apollos: I strongly urged him to come to you with the brothers, but he was not at all willing to come now. However, he will come when he has an opportunity.

FINAL EXHORTATION

¹³ Be alert, stand firm in the faith, be courageous, be strong. ¹⁴ Do everything in love.

¹⁵ Brothers and sisters, you know the household of Stephanas: They are the firstfruits of Achaia and have devoted themselves to serving the saints. I urge you ¹⁶ also to submit to such people, and to everyone who works and labors with them. ¹⁷ I am delighted to have Stephanas, Fortunatus, and

Achaicus present, because these men have made up for your absence. [18] For they have refreshed my spirit and yours. Therefore recognize such people.

CONCLUSION

[19] The churches of Asia send you greetings. Aquila and Priscilla send you greetings warmly in the Lord, along with the church that meets in their home. [20] All the brothers and sisters send you greetings. Greet one another with a holy kiss.

[21] This greeting is in my own hand—Paul. [22] If anyone does not love the Lord, a curse be on him. Our Lord, come! [23] The grace of the Lord Jesus be with you. [24] My love be with all of you in Christ Jesus.

♥ GOING DEEPER

Deuteronomy 31:6–8

[6] "Be strong and courageous; don't be terrified or afraid of them. For the LORD your God is the one who will go with you; he will not leave you or abandon you."

[7] Moses then summoned Joshua and said to him in the sight of all Israel, "Be strong and courageous, for you will go with this people into the land the LORD swore to give to their ancestors. You will enable them to take possession of it. [8] The LORD is the one who will go before you. He will be with you; he will not leave you or abandon you. Do not be afraid or discouraged."

1 Thessalonians 4:9–12

LOVING AND WORKING

[9] About brotherly love: You don't need me to write you because you yourselves are taught by God to love one another. [10] In fact, you are doing this toward all the brothers and sisters in the entire region of Macedonia. But we encourage you, brothers and sisters, to do this even more, [11] to seek to lead a quiet life, to mind your own business, and to work with your own hands, as we commanded you, [12] so that you may behave properly in the presence of outsiders and not be dependent on anyone.

2 Corinthians

But he said to me, "My grace is sufficient for you, for my power is perfected in weakness." Therefore, I will most gladly boast all the more about my weaknesses, so that Christ's power may reside in me.

2 CORINTHIANS 12:9

2 Corinthians

TIME TO READ 2 CORINTHIANS

38 Minutes

Paul wrote 2 Corinthians around AD 56, during his third missionary journey. He included more personal information about himself here than in any of his other letters.

A LITTLE BACKGROUND

First Corinthians was not well received by the church at Corinth. Timothy was sent to Corinth (1Co 4:17; 16:10), and when he returned to Paul in Ephesus, reported that the church was still greatly troubled by the arrival of false apostles in Corinth (2Co 11:4, 13–15). These were perhaps Judaizers, who asked Corinthian believers of Gentile heritage to live according to Mosaic regulations (Gl 2:14). Paul visited Corinth a second time, describing this visit as sorrowful or "painful" (2Co 2:1; 13:2).

Paul then wrote a third (now lost) severe letter of stinging rebuke to Corinth from Ephesus (2Co 2:3–4, 9). After delivering the letter to Corinth, Titus came to Paul with the news that most of the Corinthian church had repented. Paul decided to write to them one more time, in the letter now known as 2 Corinthians, expressing his relief but still pleading with an unrepentant minority. He promised to come to Corinth a third time (2Co 12:14; 13:1), which he did while on his way to Jerusalem (Ac 20:2–3).

MESSAGE & PURPOSE

Paul wrote to the Corinthian Christians to express his joy that the majority had been restored, to ask for an offering on behalf of the poor saints in Jerusalem, and to defend his ministry as an apostle to the minority of unrepentant Corinthian believers.

GIVE THANKS FOR THE BOOK OF 2 CORINTHIANS

Second Corinthians contributes to our understanding of ministry by teaching us four key truths:

- God, through Christ, is reconciling the world to Himself and has given to us a ministry of reconciliation.
- True ministry in Christ's name involves both suffering and victory.
- Serving Christ means ministering to every need of the people in His name.
- Leaders in ministry need support and trust from those to whom they minister.

The God of Comfort

As you begin 2 Corinthians, remember to keep taking notes on the practices or teachings that stand out to you.

2 Corinthians 1

GREETING

¹ Paul, an apostle of Christ Jesus by God's will, and Timothy our brother:

To the church of God at Corinth, with all the saints who are throughout Achaia.

² Grace to you and peace from God our Father and the Lord Jesus Christ.

THE GOD OF COMFORT

³ Blessed be the God and Father of our Lord Jesus Christ, the Father of mercies and the God of all comfort. ⁴ He comforts us in all our affliction, so that we may be able to comfort those who are in any kind of affliction, through the comfort we ourselves receive from God. ⁵ For just as the sufferings of Christ overflow to us, so also through Christ our comfort overflows. ⁶ If we are afflicted, it is for your comfort and salvation. If we are comforted, it is for your comfort, which produces in you patient endurance of the same sufferings that we suffer. ⁷ And our hope for you is firm, because we know that as you share in the sufferings, so you will also share in the comfort.

CONTINUED

For just as the sufferings of Christ overflow to us, so also through Christ our comfort overflows.

2 CORINTHIANS 1:5

8 We don't want you to be unaware, brothers and sisters, of our affliction that took place in Asia. We were completely overwhelmed—beyond our strength—so that we even despaired of life itself. 9 Indeed, we felt that we had received the sentence of death, so that we would not trust in ourselves but in God who raises the dead. 10 He has delivered us from such a terrible death, and he will deliver us. We have put our hope in him that he will deliver us again 11 while you join in helping us by your prayers. Then many will give thanks on our behalf for the gift that came to us through the prayers of many.

A CLEAR CONSCIENCE

12 Indeed, this is our boast: The testimony of our conscience is that we have conducted ourselves in the world, and especially toward you, with godly sincerity and purity, not by human wisdom but by God's grace. 13 For we are writing nothing to you other than what you can read and also understand. I hope you will understand completely— 14 just as you have partially understood us—that we are your reason for pride, just as you also are ours in the day of our Lord Jesus.

A VISIT POSTPONED

15 Because of this confidence, I planned to come to you first, so that you could have a second benefit, 16 and to visit you on my way to Macedonia, and then come to you again from Macedonia and be helped by you on my journey to Judea. 17 Now when I planned this, was I of two minds? Or what I plan, do I plan in a purely human way so that I say "Yes, yes" and "No, no" at the same time? 18 As God is faithful, our message to you is not "Yes and no." 19 For the Son of God, Jesus Christ, whom we proclaimed among you—Silvanus, Timothy, and I—did not become "Yes and no." On the contrary, in him it is always "Yes." 20 For every one of God's promises is "Yes" in him. Therefore, through him we also say "Amen" to the glory of God. 21 Now it is God who strengthens us together with you in Christ, and who has anointed us. 22 He has also put his seal on us and given us the Spirit in our hearts as a down payment.

23 I call on God as a witness, on my life, that it was to spare you that I did not come to Corinth. 24 I do not mean that we lord it over your faith, but we are workers with you for your joy, because you stand firm in your faith.

2 Corinthians 2:1–4

[1] In fact, I made up my mind about this: I would not come to you on another painful visit. [2] For if I cause you pain, then who will cheer me other than the one being hurt by me? [3] I wrote this very thing so that when I came I wouldn't have pain from those who ought to give me joy, because I am confident about all of you that my joy will also be yours. [4] For I wrote to you with many tears out of an extremely troubled and anguished heart—not to cause you pain, but that you should know the abundant love I have for you.

♥ GOING DEEPER

Isaiah 40:1–2

GOD'S PEOPLE COMFORTED

[1] "Comfort, comfort my people,"
says your God.
[2] "Speak tenderly to Jerusalem,
and announce to her
that her time of hard service is over,
her iniquity has been pardoned,
and she has received from the LORD's hand
double for all her sins."

Romans 5:8–10

[8] But God proves his own love for us in that while we were still sinners, Christ died for us. [9] How much more then, since we have now been justified by his blood, will we be saved through him from wrath. [10] For if, while we were enemies, we were reconciled to God through the death of his Son, then how much more, having been reconciled, will we be saved by his life.

A Sinner Forgiven

2 Corinthians 2:5–17

A SINNER FORGIVEN

⁵ If anyone has caused pain, he has caused pain not so much to me but to some degree—not to exaggerate—to all of you. ⁶ This punishment by the majority is sufficient for that person. ⁷ As a result, you should instead forgive and comfort him. Otherwise, he may be overwhelmed by excessive grief. ⁸ Therefore I urge you to reaffirm your love to him. ⁹ I wrote for this purpose: to test your character to see if you are obedient in everything. ¹⁰ Anyone you forgive, I do too. For what I have forgiven—if I have forgiven anything—it is for your benefit in the presence of Christ, ¹¹ so that we may not be taken advantage of by Satan. For we are not ignorant of his schemes.

A TRIP TO MACEDONIA

¹² When I came to Troas to preach the gospel of Christ, even though the Lord opened a door for me, ¹³ I had no rest in my spirit because I did not find my brother Titus. Instead, I said good-bye to them and left for Macedonia.

A MINISTRY OF LIFE OR DEATH

¹⁴ But thanks be to God, who always leads us in Christ's triumphal procession and through us spreads the aroma of the knowledge of him in every place. ¹⁵ For to God we are the fragrance of Christ among those who are being saved and among those who are perishing. ¹⁶ To some we are an aroma of death leading to death, but to others, an aroma of life leading to life. Who is adequate for these things? ¹⁷ For we do not market the word of God for profit like so many. On the contrary, we speak with sincerity in Christ, as from God and before God.

♥ GOING DEEPER

Psalm 32:1–2
¹ How joyful is the one
whose transgression is forgiven,
whose sin is covered!
² How joyful is a person whom

the Lord does not charge with iniquity
and in whose spirit is no deceit!

Matthew 6:14–15

[14] "For if you forgive others their offenses, your heavenly Father will forgive you as well. [15] But if you don't forgive others, your Father will not forgive your offenses."

Colossians 3:12–17

THE CHRISTIAN LIFE

[12] Therefore, as God's chosen ones, holy and dearly loved, put on compassion, kindness, humility, gentleness, and patience, [13] bearing with one another and forgiving one another if anyone has a grievance against another.

Just as the Lord has forgiven you, so you are also to forgive.

[14] Above all, put on love, which is the perfect bond of unity. [15] And let the peace of Christ, to which you were also called in one body, rule your hearts. And be thankful. [16] Let the word of Christ dwell richly among you, in all wisdom teaching and admonishing one another through psalms, hymns, and spiritual songs, singing to God with gratitude in your hearts. [17] And whatever you do, in word or in deed, do everything in the name of the Lord Jesus, giving thanks to God the Father through him.

Living Letters

2 Corinthians 3

LIVING LETTERS

¹ Are we beginning to commend ourselves again? Or do we need, like some, letters of recommendation to you or from you? ² You yourselves are our letter, written on our hearts, known and read by everyone. ³ You show that you are Christ's letter, delivered by us, not written with ink but with the Spirit of the living God—not on tablets of stone but on tablets of human hearts.

PAUL'S COMPETENCE

⁴ Such is the confidence we have through Christ before God. ⁵ It is not that we are competent in ourselves to claim anything as coming from ourselves, but our adequacy is from God. ⁶ He has made us competent to be ministers of a new covenant, not of the letter, but of the Spirit. For the letter kills, but the Spirit gives life.

NEW COVENANT MINISTRY

⁷ Now if the ministry that brought death, chiseled in letters on stones, came with glory, so that the Israelites were not able to gaze steadily at Moses's face because of its glory, which was set aside, ⁸ how will the ministry of the Spirit not be more glorious? ⁹ For if the ministry that brought condemnation had glory, the ministry that brings righteousness overflows with even more glory. ¹⁰ In fact, what had been glorious is not glorious now by comparison because of the glory that surpasses it.

¹¹ For if what was set aside was glorious, what endures will be even more glorious.

¹² Since, then, we have such a hope, we act with great boldness. ¹³ We are not like Moses, who used to put a veil over his face to prevent the Israelites from gazing steadily until the end of the glory of what was being set aside, ¹⁴ but their minds were

hardened. For to this day, at the reading of the old covenant, the same veil remains; it is not lifted, because it is set aside only in Christ. [15] Yet still today, whenever Moses is read, a veil lies over their hearts, [16] but whenever a person turns to the Lord, the veil is removed. [17] Now the Lord is the Spirit, and where the Spirit of the Lord is, there is freedom. [18] We all, with unveiled faces, are looking as in a mirror at the glory of the Lord and are being transformed into the same image from glory to glory; this is from the Lord who is the Spirit.

GOING DEEPER

Jeremiah 31:31–34

THE NEW COVENANT

[31] "Look, the days are coming"—this is the LORD's declaration—"when I will make a new covenant with the house of Israel and with the house of Judah. [32] This one will not be like the covenant I made with their ancestors on the day I took them by the hand to lead them out of the land of Egypt—my covenant that they broke even though I am their master"—the LORD's declaration. [33] "Instead, this is the covenant I will make with the house of Israel after those days"—the LORD's declaration. "I will put my teaching within them and write it on their hearts. I will be their God, and they will be my people. [34] No longer will one teach his neighbor or his brother, saying, 'Know the LORD,' for they will all know me, from the least to the greatest of them"—this is the LORD's declaration. "For I will forgive their iniquity and never again remember their sin."

1 John 3:2

Dear friends, we are God's children now, and what we will be has not yet been revealed. We know that when he appears, we will be like him because we will see him as he is.

Week Four

Look back through any notes you made this week as you answer the following questions.

1   What aspects of the Corinthian church surprised you?
       What parts of their lives were confusing or different?

2   What teachings from this week's reading challenged you as a member of the body of Christ?

3   How would you like to practice those teachings in your own community this week?

NOTES

Grace

DAY 27

Day

Take this day to catch up on your
reading, pray, and rest in the
presence of the Lord.

Therefore we were buried
with him by baptism into
death, in order that, just
as Christ was raised from
the dead by the glory of the
Father, so we too may walk
in newness of life.

ROMANS 6:4

Weekly Truth

Scripture is God-breathed and true. When we memorize it, we carry the good news of Jesus with us wherever we go.

Now that we're reading 2 Corinthians, we'll memorize our key verse for this letter, 2 Corinthians 12:9. We'll start with the first half of the verse, remembering the grace of Christ that always covers us.

But he said to me, "My grace is sufficient for you, for my power is perfected in weakness." Therefore, I will most gladly boast all the more about my weaknesses, so that Christ's power may reside in me.

2 CORINTHIANS 12:9

See tips for memorizing Scripture on page 156.

Laci Fowler, *Late Summer Blooms*, mixed media on canvas, 22x28 in.

Week Five

The Light of the Gospel

2 Corinthians 4

THE LIGHT OF THE GOSPEL

¹ Therefore, since we have this ministry because we were shown mercy, we do not give up. ² Instead, we have renounced secret and shameful things, not acting deceitfully or distorting the word of God, but commending ourselves before God to everyone's conscience by an open display of the truth. ³ But if our gospel is veiled, it is veiled to those who are perishing. ⁴ In their case, the god of this age has blinded the minds of the unbelievers to keep them from seeing the light of the gospel of the glory of Christ, who is the image of God. ⁵ For we are not proclaiming ourselves but Jesus Christ as Lord, and ourselves as your servants for Jesus's sake. ⁶ For God who said, "Let light shine out of darkness," has shone in our hearts to give the light of the knowledge of God's glory in the face of Jesus Christ.

TREASURE IN CLAY JARS

⁷ Now we have this treasure in clay jars, so that this extraordinary power may be from God and not

from us. [8] We are afflicted in every way but not crushed; we are perplexed but not in despair; [9] we are persecuted but not abandoned; we are struck down but not destroyed. [10] We always carry the death of Jesus in our body, so that the life of Jesus may also be displayed in our body. [11] For we who live are always being given over to death for Jesus's sake, so that Jesus's life may also be displayed in our mortal flesh. [12] So then, death is at work in us, but life in you. [13] And since we have the same spirit of faith in keeping with what is written, I believed, therefore I spoke, we also believe, and therefore speak. [14] For we know that the one who raised the Lord Jesus will also raise us with Jesus and present us with you. [15] Indeed, everything is for your benefit so that, as grace extends through more and more people, it may cause thanksgiving to increase to the glory of God.

[16] Therefore we do not give up. Even though our outer person is being destroyed, our inner person is being renewed day by day. [17] For our momentary light affliction is producing for us an absolutely incomparable eternal weight of glory. [18] So we do not focus on what is seen, but on what is unseen. For what is seen is temporary, but what is unseen is eternal.

♥ GOING DEEPER

Isaiah 9:2–7
[2] The people walking in darkness
have seen a great light;

a light has dawned on those living in the land of darkness.

[3] You have enlarged the nation
and increased its joy.
The people have rejoiced before you
as they rejoice at harvest time
and as they rejoice when dividing spoils.
[4] For you have shattered their oppressive yoke
and the rod on their shoulders,
the staff of their oppressor,
just as you did on the day of Midian.
[5] For every trampling boot of battle
and the bloodied garments of war
will be burned as fuel for the fire.
[6] For a child will be born for us,
a son will be given to us,
and the government will be on his shoulders.
He will be named
Wonderful Counselor, Mighty God,
Eternal Father, Prince of Peace.
[7] The dominion will be vast,
and its prosperity will never end.
He will reign on the throne of David
and over his kingdom,
to establish and sustain it
with justice and righteousness from now on and forever.
The zeal of the LORD of Armies will accomplish this.

Matthew 5:14–16
[14] "You are the light of the world. A city situated on a hill cannot be hidden. [15] No one lights a lamp and puts it under a basket, but rather on a lampstand, and it gives light for all who are in the house. [16] In the same way, let your light shine before others, so that they may see your good works and give glory to your Father in heaven."

Our Future After Death

2 Corinthians 5

OUR FUTURE AFTER DEATH

[1] For we know that if our earthly tent we live in is destroyed, we have a building from God, an eternal dwelling in the heavens, not made with hands. [2] Indeed, we groan in this tent, desiring to put on our heavenly dwelling, [3] since, when we are clothed, we will not be found naked. [4] Indeed, we groan while we are in this tent, burdened as we are, because we do not want to be unclothed but clothed, so that mortality may be swallowed up by life. [5] Now the one who prepared us for this very purpose is God, who gave us the Spirit as a down payment.

[6] So we are always confident and know that while we are at home in the body we are away from the Lord. [7] For we walk by faith, not by sight. [8] In fact, we are confident, and we would prefer to be away from the body and at home with the Lord. [9] Therefore, whether we are at home or away, we make it our aim to be pleasing to him. [10] For we must all appear before the judgment seat of Christ, so that each may be repaid for what he has done in the body, whether good or evil.

[11] Therefore, since we know the fear of the Lord, we try to persuade people. What we are is plain to God, and I hope it is also plain to your consciences. [12] We are not commending ourselves to you again, but giving you an opportunity to be proud of us, so that you may have a reply for those who take pride in outward appearance rather than in the heart. [13] For if we are out of our mind, it is for God; if we are in our right mind, it is for you. [14] For the love of Christ compels us, since we have reached this conclusion, that one died for all, and therefore all died. [15] And he died for all so that those who live should no longer live for themselves, but for the one who died for them and was raised.

THE MINISTRY OF RECONCILIATION

[16] From now on, then, we do not know anyone from a worldly perspective. Even if we have known Christ from a worldly perspective, yet now we no longer know him in this way. [17] Therefore, if anyone is in Christ, he is a new creation; the old has passed away, and see, the new has come! [18] Everything is from God, who has reconciled us to himself through Christ and has given us the ministry of reconciliation. [19] That is, in Christ, God was reconciling the world to himself, not counting their trespasses against them, and he has committed the message of reconciliation to us.

²⁰ Therefore, we are ambassadors for Christ, since God is making his appeal through us. We plead on Christ's behalf, "Be reconciled to God." ²¹ He made the one who did not know sin to be sin for us, so that in him we might become the righteousness of God.

2 Corinthians 6:1–2

¹ Working together with him, we also appeal to you, "Don't receive the grace of God in vain." ² For he says:

> At an acceptable time I listened to you,
> and in the day of salvation I helped you.

See, now is the acceptable time; now is the day of salvation!

♥ GOING DEEPER

Psalm 27:4–5

⁴ I have asked one thing from the LORD;
it is what I desire:
to dwell in the house of the LORD
all the days of my life,
gazing on the beauty of the LORD
and seeking him in his temple.
⁵ For he will conceal me in his shelter
in the day of adversity;
he will hide me under the cover of his tent;
he will set me high on a rock.

1 Thessalonians 4:13–18

THE COMFORT OF CHRIST'S COMING

¹³ We do not want you to be uninformed, brothers and sisters, concerning those who are asleep, so that you will not grieve like the rest, who have no hope. ¹⁴ For if we believe that Jesus died and rose again, in the same way, through Jesus, God will bring with him those who have fallen asleep. ¹⁵ For we say this to you by a word from the Lord: We who are still alive at the Lord's coming will certainly not precede those who have fallen asleep. ¹⁶ For the Lord himself will descend from heaven with a shout, with the archangel's voice, and with the trumpet of God, and the dead in Christ will rise first. ¹⁷ Then we who are still alive, who are left, will be caught up together with them in the clouds to meet the Lord in the air, and so we will always be with the Lord. ¹⁸ Therefore encourage one another with these words.

DAY 31

God's Ministers

2 Corinthians 6:3–18

THE CHARACTER OF PAUL'S MINISTRY

³ We are not giving anyone an occasion for offense, so that the ministry will not be blamed. ⁴ Instead, as God's ministers, we commend ourselves in everything: by great endurance, by afflictions, by hardships, by difficulties, ⁵ by beatings, by imprisonments, by riots, by labors, by sleepless nights, by times of hunger, ⁶ by purity, by knowledge, by patience, by kindness, by the Holy Spirit, by sincere love, ⁷ by the word of truth, by the power of God; through weapons of righteousness for the right hand and the left, ⁸ through glory and dishonor, through slander and good report; regarded as deceivers, yet true; ⁹ as unknown, yet recognized; as dying, yet see—we live; as being disciplined, yet not killed; ¹⁰ as grieving, yet always rejoicing; as poor, yet enriching many; as having nothing, yet possessing everything. ¹¹ We have spoken openly to you, Corinthians; our heart has been opened wide. ¹² We are not withholding our affection from you, but you are withholding yours from us. ¹³ I speak as to my children; as a proper response, open your heart to us.

SEPARATION TO GOD

¹⁴ Do not be yoked together with those who do not believe. For what partnership is there between righteousness and lawlessness? Or what fellowship does light have with darkness? ¹⁵ What agreement does Christ have with Belial? Or what does a believer have in common with an unbeliever? ¹⁶ And what agreement does the temple of God have with idols? For we are the temple of the living God, as God said:

I will dwell
and walk among them,
and I will be their God,
and they will be my people.
¹⁷ Therefore, come out from among them
and be separate, says the Lord;
do not touch any unclean thing,
and I will welcome you.
¹⁸ And I will be a Father to you,
and you will be sons and daughters to me,
says the Lord Almighty.

2 Corinthians 7:1

So then, dear friends, since we have these promises, let us cleanse ourselves from every impurity of the flesh and spirit, bringing holiness to completion in the fear of God.

GOING DEEPER

Micah 6:8

Mankind, he has told each of you what is good
and what it is the LORD requires of you:
to act justly,
to love faithfulness,
and to walk humbly with your God.

Philippians 2:12–17

LIGHTS IN THE WORLD

[12] Therefore, my dear friends, just as you have always obeyed, so now, not only in my presence but even more in my absence, work out your own salvation with fear and trembling. [13] For it is God who is working in you both to will and to work according to his good purpose. [14] Do everything without grumbling and arguing, [15] so that you may be blameless and pure, children of God who are faultless in a crooked and perverted generation, among whom

you shine like stars in the world, [16] by holding firm to the word of life.

Then I can boast in the day of Christ that I didn't run or labor for nothing. [17] But even if I am poured out as a drink offering on the sacrificial service of your faith, I am glad and rejoice with all of you.

NOTES

What Is the Church?

Throughout the New Testament, different metaphors for the Church are used to help us understand what the community of believers is and how it is meant to function. Included here are some of the images used in the New Testament to describe the Church.

THE BODY OF CHRIST

As it is, there are many parts, but one body.	1CO 12:20
Now you are the body of Christ, and individual members of it.	1CO 12:27
To equip the saints for the work of ministry, to build up the body of Christ.	EPH 4:12
He is also the head of the body, the church.	COL 1:18

THE BRIDE OF CHRIST

I have promised you in marriage to one husband—to present a pure virgin to Christ.	2CO 11:2
Husbands, love your wives, just as Christ loved the church and gave himself for her to make her holy...	EPH 5:25–26
The marriage of the Lamb has come, and his bride has prepared herself.	RV 19:7

THE FAMILY OF GOD

"Whoever does the will of my Father in heaven is my brother and sister and mother."	MT 12:50
We are God's children, and if children, also heirs—heirs of God and coheirs with Christ.	RM 8:16–17
"And I will be a Father to you, and you will be sons and daughters to me."	2CO 6:18
Let us work for the good of all, especially for those who belong to the household of faith.	GL 6:10
See what great love the Father has given us that we should be called God's children—and we are!	1JN 3:1

THE FLOCK

LK 12:32 — "Don't be afraid, little flock, because your Father delights to give you the kingdom."

JN 10:11 — "I am the good shepherd. The good shepherd lays down his life for the sheep."

AC 20:28 — Be on guard for yourselves and for all the flock of which the Holy Spirit has appointed you as overseers, to shepherd the church of God.

HEB 13:20 — Our Lord Jesus—the great Shepherd of the sheep...

THE HOUSE OF GOD/CHRIST

EPH 2:19 — You are no longer foreigners and strangers, but fellow citizens with the saints, and members of God's household.

1TM 3:15 — ...God's household, which is the church of the living God, the pillar and foundation of truth.

HEB 3:6 — Christ was faithful as a Son over his household. And we are that household...

1PT 2:5 — You yourselves, as living stones, a spiritual house, are being built to be a holy priesthood.

THE LAMPSTAND/THE LIGHT OF THE WORLD

MT 5:14 — "You are the light of the world. A city situated on a hill cannot be hidden."

RV 1:20 — "...the seven lampstands are the seven churches."

THE LETTERS

2CO 3:3 — You show that you are Christ's letter, delivered by us, not written with ink but with the Spirit of the living God—not on tablets of stone but on tablets of human hearts.

THE PEOPLE OF GOD

PHP 3:20 — Our citizenship is in heaven.

1PT 2:9 — But you are a chosen race, a royal priesthood, a holy nation, a people for his possession...

RV 1:6 — ...and made us a kingdom, priests to his God and Father...

RV 21:3 — They will be his peoples, and God himself will be with them and will be their God.

THE TEMPLE OF THE SPIRIT

1CO 3:16 — Don't you yourselves know that you are God's temple and that the Spirit of God lives in you?

2CO 6:16 — For we are the temple of the living God.

EPH 2:22 — In him you are also being built together for God's dwelling in the Spirit.

DAY 32

Joy and Repentance

2 Corinthians 7:2–16

JOY AND REPENTANCE

² Make room for us in your hearts. We have wronged no one, corrupted no one, taken advantage of no one. ³ I don't say this to condemn you, since I have already said that you are in our hearts, to die together and to live together. ⁴ I am very frank with you; I have great pride in you. I am filled with encouragement; I am overflowing with joy in all our afflictions.

⁵ In fact, when we came into Macedonia, we had no rest. Instead, we were troubled in every way: conflicts on the outside, fears within. ⁶ But God, who comforts the downcast, comforted us by the arrival of Titus, ⁷ and not only by his arrival but also by the comfort he received from you. He told us about your deep longing, your sorrow, and your zeal for me, so that I rejoiced even more. ⁸ For even if I grieved you with my letter, I don't regret it. And if I regretted it—since I saw that the letter grieved you, yet only for a while— ⁹ I now rejoice, not because you were grieved, but because your grief led to repentance. For you were grieved as

God willed, so that you didn't experience any loss from us. ¹⁰ For godly grief produces a repentance that leads to salvation without regret, but worldly grief produces death. ¹¹ For consider how much diligence this very thing—this grieving as God wills—has produced in you: what a desire to clear yourselves, what indignation, what fear, what deep longing, what zeal, what justice! In every way you showed yourselves to be pure in this matter. ¹² So even though I wrote to you, it was not because of the one who did wrong, or because of the one who was wronged, but in order that your devotion to us might be made plain to you in the sight of God. ¹³ For this reason we have been comforted.

In addition to our own comfort, we rejoiced even more over the joy Titus had, because his spirit was refreshed by all of you. ¹⁴ For if I have made any boast to him about you, I have not been disappointed; but as I have spoken everything to you in truth, so our boasting to Titus has also turned out to be the truth. ¹⁵ And his affection toward you is even greater as he remembers the obedience of all of you, and how you received him with fear and trembling. [16] I rejoice that I have complete confidence in you.

◆ GOING DEEPER

Lamentations 3:19–24

ז ZAYIN

[19] Remember my affliction and my homelessness,
the wormwood and the poison.
[20] I continually remember them
and have become depressed.
[21] Yet I call this to mind,
and therefore I have hope:

ח CHETH

[22] Because of the LORD's
faithful love
we do not perish,
for his mercies never end.

[23] They are new every morning;
great is your faithfulness!
[24] I say, "The LORD is my portion,
therefore I will put my hope in him."

Acts 3:19–20

[19] Therefore repent and turn back, so that your sins may be wiped out, [20] that seasons of refreshing may come from the presence of the Lord, and that he may send Jesus, who has been appointed for you as the Messiah.

The Collection

2 Corinthians 8

APPEAL TO COMPLETE THE COLLECTION

[1] We want you to know, brothers and sisters, about the grace of God that was given to the churches of Macedonia: [2] During a severe trial brought about by affliction, their abundant joy and their extreme poverty overflowed in a wealth of generosity on their part. [3] I can testify that, according to their ability and even beyond their ability, of their own accord, [4] they begged us earnestly for the privilege of sharing in the ministry to the saints, [5] and not just as we had hoped. Instead, they gave themselves first to the Lord and then to us by God's will. [6] So we urged Titus that just as he had begun, so he should also complete among you this act of grace.

[7] Now as you excel in everything—in faith, speech, knowledge, and in all diligence, and in your love for us—excel also in this act of grace. [8] I am not saying this as a command. Rather, by means of the diligence of others, I am testing the genuineness of your love. [9] For you know the grace of our Lord Jesus Christ: Though he was rich, for your sake he became poor, so that by his poverty you might become rich. [10] And in this matter I am giving advice because it is profitable for you, who began last year not only to do something but also to want to do it. [11] Now also finish the task, so that just as there was an eager desire, there may also be a completion, according to what you have. [12] For if the eagerness is there, the gift is acceptable according to what a person has, not according to what he does not have. [13] It is not that there should be relief for others and hardship for you, but it is a question of equality. [14] At the present time your surplus is available for their need, so that their abundance may in turn meet your need, in order that there may be equality. [15] As it is written: The person who had much did not have too much, and the person who had little did not have too little.

CONTINUED

For you know the grace of our Lord Jesus Christ: Though he was rich, for your sake he became poor, so that by his poverty you might become rich.

2 CORINTHIANS 8:9

¹⁶ Thanks be to God, who put the same concern for you into the heart of Titus. ¹⁷ For he welcomed our appeal and, being very diligent, went out to you by his own choice. ¹⁸ We have sent with him the brother who is praised among all the churches for his gospel ministry. ¹⁹ And not only that, but he was also appointed by the churches to accompany us with this gracious gift that we are administering for the glory of the Lord himself and to show our eagerness to help. ²⁰ We are taking this precaution so that no one will criticize us about this large sum that we are administering. ²¹ Indeed, we are giving careful thought to do what is right, not only before the Lord but also before people. ²² We have also sent with them our brother. We have often tested him in many circumstances and found him to be diligent—and now even more diligent because of his great confidence in you. ²³ As for Titus, he is my partner and coworker for you; as for our brothers, they are the messengers of the churches, the glory of Christ. ²⁴ Therefore, show them proof before the churches of your love and of our boasting about you.

❤ GOING DEEPER

Acts 2:42–47

A GENEROUS AND GROWING CHURCH

⁴² They devoted themselves to the apostles' teaching, to the fellowship, to the breaking of bread, and to prayer.

⁴³ Everyone was filled with awe, and many wonders and signs were being performed through the apostles. ⁴⁴ Now all the believers were together and held all things in common. ⁴⁵ They sold their possessions and property and distributed the proceeds to all, as any had need. ⁴⁶ Every day they devoted themselves to meeting together in the temple, and broke bread from house to house. They ate their food with joyful and sincere hearts, ⁴⁷ praising God and enjoying the favor of all the people. Every day the Lord added to their number those who were being saved.

Philippians 2:4–11

⁴ Everyone should look not to his own interests, but rather to the interests of others.

CHRIST'S HUMILITY AND EXALTATION

⁵ Adopt the same attitude as that of Christ Jesus,

⁶ who, existing in the form of God,
did not consider equality with God
as something to be exploited.
⁷ Instead he emptied himself
by assuming the form of a servant,
taking on the likeness of humanity.
And when he had come as a man,
⁸ he humbled himself by
    becoming obedient
to the point of death—
even to death on a cross.
⁹ For this reason God highly exalted him
and gave him the name
that is above every name,
¹⁰ so that at the name of Jesus
every knee will bow—
in heaven and on earth
and under the earth—
¹¹ and every tongue will confess
that Jesus Christ is Lord,
to the glory of God the Father.

Week Five

Look back through any notes you made this week as you answer the following questions.

1 What aspects of the Corinthian church surprised you?
What parts of their lives were confusing or different?

2 What teachings from this week's reading challenged you as a member of the body of Christ?

3 How would you like to practice those teachings in your own community this week?

NOTES

Grace

DAY 34

Day

Take this day to catch up on your reading, pray, and rest in the presence of the Lord.

Because of the Lord's faithful love we do not perish, for his mercies never end. They are new every morning; great is your faithfulness! I say, "The Lord is my portion, therefore I will put my hope in him."

LAMENTATIONS 3:22–24

Weekly Truth

Scripture is God-breathed and true. When we memorize it,
we carry the good news of Jesus with us wherever we go.

This week, we're continuing to memorize 2 Corinthians 12:9
by adding the second part of the verse.

But he said to me, "My grace is sufficient for you, for my power is perfected in weakness." Therefore, I will most gladly boast all the more about my weaknesses, so that Christ's power may reside in me.

2 CORINTHIANS 12:9

See tips for memorizing Scripture on page 156.

Laci Fowler, *Rosa*, mixed media on canvas, 36x36 in.

Week Six

Motivations for Giving

2 Corinthians 9
MOTIVATIONS FOR GIVING

¹ Now concerning the ministry to the saints, it is unnecessary for me to write to you. ² For I know your eagerness, and I boast about you to the Macedonians, "Achaia has been ready since last year," and your zeal has stirred up most of them. ³ But I am sending the brothers so that our boasting about you in this matter would not prove empty, and so that you would be ready just as I said. ⁴ Otherwise, if any Macedonians come with me and find you unprepared, we, not to mention you, would be put to shame in that situation. ⁵ Therefore I considered it necessary to urge the brothers to go on ahead to you and arrange in advance the generous gift you promised, so that it will be ready as a gift and not as an extortion.

⁶ The point is this: The person who sows sparingly will also reap sparingly, and the person who sows generously will also reap generously. ⁷ Each person should do as he has decided in his heart—not reluctantly or out of compulsion, since God loves a cheerful giver.

8 And God is able to make every grace overflow to you,

so that in every way, always having everything you need, you may excel in every good work. 9 As it is written:

> He distributed freely;
> he gave to the poor;
> his righteousness endures forever.

10 Now the one who provides seed for the sower and bread for food will also provide and multiply your seed and increase the harvest of your righteousness. 11 You will be enriched in every way for all generosity, which produces thanksgiving to God through us. 12 For the ministry of this service is not only supplying the needs of the saints but is also overflowing in many expressions of thanks to God. 13 Because of the proof provided by this ministry, they will glorify God for your obedient confession of the gospel of Christ, and for your generosity in sharing with them and with everyone. 14 And as they pray on your behalf, they will have deep affection for you because of the surpassing grace of God in you. 15 Thanks be to God for his indescribable gift!

◆ GOING DEEPER

Psalm 126
ZION'S RESTORATION

A song of ascents.

1 When the LORD restored the fortunes of Zion,
we were like those who dream.
2 Our mouths were filled with laughter then,
and our tongues with shouts of joy.
Then they said among the nations,
"The LORD has done great things for them."
3 The LORD had done great things for us;
we were joyful.

[4] Restore our fortunes, Lord,
like watercourses in the Negev.
[5] Those who sow in tears
will reap with shouts of joy.
[6] Though one goes along weeping,
carrying the bag of seed,
he will surely come back with shouts of joy,
carrying his sheaves.

Hosea 10:12

Sow righteousness for yourselves
and reap faithful love;
break up your unplowed ground.
It is time to seek the Lord
until he comes and sends righteousness
on you like the rain.

Boast in the Lord

2 Corinthians 10

PAUL'S APOSTOLIC AUTHORITY

¹ Now I, Paul, myself, appeal to you by the meekness and gentleness of Christ—I who am humble among you in person but bold toward you when absent. ² I beg you that when I am present I will not need to be bold with the confidence by which I plan to challenge certain people who think we are living according to the flesh. ³ For although we live in the flesh, we do not wage war according to the flesh, ⁴ since the weapons of our warfare are not of the flesh, but are powerful through God for the demolition of strongholds. We demolish arguments ⁵ and every proud thing that is raised up against the knowledge of God, and we take every thought captive to obey Christ. ⁶ And we are ready to punish any disobedience, once your obedience is complete.

⁷ Look at what is obvious. If anyone is confident that he belongs to Christ, let him remind himself of this: Just as he belongs to Christ, so do we. ⁸ For if I boast a little too much about our authority, which the Lord gave for building you up and not for tearing you down, I will not be put to shame. ⁹ I don't want to seem as though I am trying to terrify you with my letters. ¹⁰ For it is said, "His letters are weighty and powerful, but his physical presence is weak and his public speaking amounts to nothing." ¹¹ Let such a person consider this: What we are in our letters, when we are absent, we will also be in our actions when we are present.

¹² For we don't dare classify or compare ourselves with some who commend themselves. But in measuring themselves by themselves and comparing themselves to themselves, they lack understanding. ¹³ We, however, will not boast beyond measure but according to the measure of the area of ministry that God has assigned to us, which reaches even to you. ¹⁴ For we are not overextending ourselves, as if we had not reached you, since we have come to you with the gospel of Christ. ¹⁵ We are not boasting beyond measure

about other people's labors. On the contrary, we have the hope that as your faith increases, our area of ministry will be greatly enlarged, [16] so that we may preach the gospel to the regions beyond you without boasting about what has already been done in someone else's area of ministry. [17] So let the one who boasts, boast in the Lord. [18] For it is not the one commending himself who is approved, but the one the Lord commends.

◗ GOING DEEPER

Jeremiah 9:23–24
BOAST IN THE LORD

[23] "This is what the LORD says:

> The wise person should not boast in his wisdom;
> the strong should not boast in his strength;
> the wealthy should not boast in his wealth.

[24] But the one who boasts
should boast in this:
that he understands
and knows me—
that I am the LORD,
showing faithful love,
justice, and righteousness
on the earth,

> for I delight in these things.
> This is the LORD's declaration."

Ephesians 2:8–9
[8] For you are saved by grace through faith, and this is not from yourselves; it is God's gift— [9] not from works, so that no one can boast.

Paul's Sufferings for Christ

2 Corinthians 11

PAUL AND THE FALSE APOSTLES

[1] I wish you would put up with a little foolishness from me. Yes, do put up with me! [2] For I am jealous for you with a godly jealousy, because I have promised you in marriage to one husband—to present a pure virgin to Christ. [3] But I fear that, as the serpent deceived Eve by his cunning, your minds may be seduced from a sincere and pure devotion to Christ. [4] For if a person comes and preaches another Jesus, whom we did not preach, or you receive a different spirit, which you had not received, or a different gospel, which you had not accepted, you put up with it splendidly!

[5] Now I consider myself in no way inferior to those "super-apostles." [6] Even if I am untrained in public speaking, I am certainly not untrained in knowledge. Indeed, we have in every way made that clear to you in everything. [7] Or did I commit a sin by humbling myself so that you might be exalted, because I preached the gospel of God to you free of charge? [8] I robbed other churches by taking pay from them to minister to you. [9] When I was present with you and in need, I did not burden anyone, since the brothers who came from Macedonia supplied my needs. I have kept myself, and will keep myself, from burdening you in any way. [10] As the truth of Christ is in me, this boasting of mine will not be stopped in the regions of Achaia. [11] Why? Because I don't love you? God knows I do!

[12] But I will continue to do what I am doing, in order to deny an opportunity to those who want to be regarded as our equals in what they boast about. [13] For such people are false apostles, deceitful workers, disguising themselves as apostles of Christ. [14] And no wonder! For Satan disguises himself as an angel of light. [15] So it is no great surprise if his servants also disguise themselves as servants of righteousness. Their end will be according to their works.

CONTINUED

If boasting is
necessary, I will
boast about my
weaknesses.

2 CORINTHIANS 11:30

[16] I repeat: Let no one consider me a fool. But if you do, at least accept me as a fool so that I can also boast a little. [17] What I am saying in this matter of boasting, I don't speak as the Lord would, but as it were, foolishly. [18] Since many boast according to the flesh, I will also boast. [19] For you, being so wise, gladly put up with fools! [20] In fact, you put up with it if someone enslaves you, if someone exploits you, if someone takes advantage of you, if someone is arrogant toward you, if someone slaps you in the face. [21] I say this to our shame: We have been too weak for that!

But in whatever anyone dares to boast—I am talking foolishly—I also dare: [22] Are they Hebrews? So am I. Are they Israelites? So am I. Are they the descendants of Abraham? So am I. [23] Are they servants of Christ? I'm talking like a madman—I'm a better one: with far more labors, many more imprisonments, far worse beatings, many times near death.

[24] Five times I received the forty lashes minus one from the Jews. [25] Three times I was beaten with rods. Once I received a stoning. Three times I was shipwrecked. I have spent a night and a day in the open sea. [26] On frequent journeys, I faced dangers from rivers, dangers from robbers, dangers from my own people, dangers from Gentiles, dangers in the city, dangers in the wilderness, dangers at sea, and dangers among false brothers; [27] toil and hardship, many sleepless nights, hunger and thirst, often without food, cold, and without clothing. [28] Not to mention other things, there is the daily pressure on me: my concern for all the churches. [29] Who is weak, and I am not weak? Who is made to stumble, and I do not burn with indignation?

[30] If boasting is necessary, I will boast about my weaknesses. [31] The God and Father of the Lord Jesus, who is blessed forever, knows I am not lying. [32] In Damascus, a ruler under King Aretas guarded the city of Damascus in order to arrest me. [33] So I was let down in a basket through a window in the wall and escaped from his hands.

♥ **GOING DEEPER**

John 15:18–25
PERSECUTIONS PREDICTED

[18] "If the world hates you, understand that it hated me before it hated you. [19] If you were of the world, the world would love you as its own. However, because you are not of the world, but I have chosen you out of it, the world hates you. [20] Remember the word I spoke to you: 'A servant is not greater than his master.' If they persecuted me, they will also persecute you. If they kept my word, they will also keep yours. [21] But they will do all these things to you on account of my name, because they don't know the one who sent me. [22] If I had not come and spoken to them, they would not be guilty of sin. Now they have no excuse for their sin. [23] The one who hates me also hates my Father. [24] If I had not done the works among them that no one else has done, they would not be guilty of sin. Now they have seen and hated both me and my Father. [25] But this happened so that the statement written in their law might be fulfilled: They hated me for no reason."

Romans 8:18–25
FROM GROANS TO GLORY

[18] For I consider that the sufferings of this present time are not worth comparing with the glory that is going to be revealed to us. [19] For the creation eagerly waits with anticipation for God's sons to be revealed. [20] For the creation was subjected to futility—not willingly, but because of him who subjected it—in the hope [21] that the creation itself will also be set free from the bondage to decay into the glorious freedom of God's children. [22] For we know that the whole creation has been groaning together with labor pains until now. [23] Not only that, but we ourselves who have the Spirit as the firstfruits—we also groan within ourselves, eagerly waiting for adoption, the redemption of our bodies. [24] Now in this hope we were saved, but hope that is seen is not hope, because who hopes for what he sees? [25] Now if we hope for what we do not see, we eagerly wait for it with patience.

Sufficient Grace

2 Corinthians 12

SUFFICIENT GRACE

[1] Boasting is necessary. It is not profitable, but I will move on to visions and revelations of the Lord. [2] I know a man in Christ who was caught up to the third heaven fourteen years ago. Whether he was in the body or out of the body, I don't know; God knows. [3] I know that this man—whether in the body or out of the body I don't know; God knows— [4] was caught up into paradise and heard inexpressible words, which a human being is not allowed to speak. [5] I will boast about this person, but not about myself, except of my weaknesses.

[6] For if I want to boast, I wouldn't be a fool, because I would be telling the truth. But I will spare you, so that no one can credit me with something beyond what he sees in me or hears from me, [7] especially because of the extraordinary revelations. Therefore, so that I would not exalt myself, a thorn in the flesh was given to me, a messenger of Satan to torment me so that I would not exalt myself. [8] Concerning this, I pleaded with the Lord three times that it would leave me. [9] But he said to me, "My grace is sufficient for you, for my power is perfected in weakness."

Therefore, I will most gladly boast all the more about my weaknesses, so that Christ's power may reside in me. [10] So I take pleasure in weaknesses, insults, hardships, persecutions, and in difficulties, for the sake of Christ. For when I am weak, then I am strong.

SIGNS OF AN APOSTLE

[11] I have been a fool; you forced it on me. You ought to have commended me, since I am not in any way inferior to those "super-apostles," even though I am nothing. [12] The signs of an apostle were performed with unfailing endurance among you, including signs and wonders and miracles. [13] So in what way are you worse off than the other churches, except that I personally did not burden you? Forgive me for this wrong!

PAUL'S CONCERN FOR THE CORINTHIANS

[14] Look, I am ready to come to you this third time. I will not burden you, since I am not seeking what is yours, but you. For children ought not save up for their parents, but parents for their children. [15] I will most gladly spend and be spent for you. If I love you more, am I to be loved less? [16] Now granted, I did not burden you; yet sly as I am, I took you in by deceit! [17] Did I take advantage of you by any of those I sent you? [18] I urged Titus to go, and I sent the brother with him. Titus didn't take advantage of you, did he? Didn't we walk in the same spirit and in the same footsteps?

[19] Have you been thinking all along that we were defending ourselves to you? No, in the sight of God we are speaking in Christ, and everything, dear friends, is for building you up. [20] For I fear that perhaps when I come I will not find you to be what I want, and you may not find me to be what you want. Perhaps there will be quarreling, jealousy, angry outbursts, selfish ambitions, slander, gossip, arrogance, and disorder. [21] I fear that when I come my God will again humiliate me in your presence, and I will grieve for many who sinned before and have not repented of the moral impurity, sexual immorality, and sensuality they practiced.

GOING DEEPER

Mark 14:32–36

THE PRAYER IN THE GARDEN

[32] Then they came to a place named Gethsemane, and he told his disciples, "Sit here while I pray." [33] He took Peter, James, and John with him, and he began to be deeply distressed and troubled. [34] He said to them, "I am deeply grieved to the point of death. Remain here and stay awake." [35] He went a little farther, fell to the ground, and prayed that if it were possible, the hour might pass from him. [36] And he said, "Abba, Father! All things are possible for you. Take this cup away from me. Nevertheless, not what I will, but what you will."

Philippians 4:10–13

APPRECIATION OF SUPPORT

[10] I rejoiced in the Lord greatly because once again you renewed your care for me. You were, in fact, concerned about me but lacked the opportunity to show it. [11] I don't say this out of need, for I have learned to be content in whatever circumstances I find myself. [12] I know how to make do with little, and I know how to make do with a lot. In any and all circumstances I have learned the secret of being content—whether well fed or hungry, whether in abundance or in need. [13] I am able to do all things through him who strengthens me.

Finally, Rejoice

2 Corinthians 13
FINAL WARNINGS AND EXHORTATIONS

¹ This is the third time I am coming to you. Every matter must be established by the testimony of two or three witnesses. ² I gave a warning when I was present the second time, and now I give a warning while I am absent to those who sinned before and to all the rest: If I come again, I will not be lenient, ³ since you seek proof of Christ speaking in me. He is not weak in dealing with you, but powerful among you. ⁴ For he was crucified in weakness, but he lives by the power of God. For we also are weak in him, but in dealing with you we will live with him by God's power.

⁵ Test yourselves to see if you are in the faith. Examine yourselves. Or do you yourselves not recognize that Jesus Christ is in you?—unless you fail the test. ⁶ And I hope you will recognize that we ourselves do not fail the test. ⁷ But we pray to God that you do nothing wrong—not that we may appear to pass the test, but that you may do what is right, even though we may appear to fail. ⁸ For we can't do anything against the truth, but only for the truth.

⁹ We rejoice when we are weak and you are strong.

We also pray that you become fully mature. ¹⁰ This is why I am writing these things while absent, so that when I am there I may not have to deal harshly with you, in keeping with the authority the Lord gave me for building up and not for tearing down.

¹¹ Finally, brothers and sisters, rejoice. Become mature, be encouraged, be of the same mind, be at peace, and the God of love and peace will be with you. ¹² Greet one another with a holy kiss. All the saints send you greetings.

[13] The grace of the Lord Jesus Christ, and the love of God, and the fellowship of the Holy Spirit be with you all.

🛡 GOING DEEPER

Psalm 119:9–16

[9] How can a young man keep his way pure?
By keeping your word.
[10] I have sought you with all my heart;
don't let me wander from your commands.
[11] I have treasured your word in my heart
so that I may not sin against you.
[12] LORD, may you be blessed;
teach me your statutes.
[13] With my lips I proclaim
all the judgments from your mouth.
[14] I rejoice in the way revealed by your decrees
as much as in all riches.
[15] I will meditate on your precepts
and think about your ways.
[16] I will delight in your statutes;
I will not forget your word.

Colossians 1:9–12

PRAYER FOR SPIRITUAL GROWTH

[9] For this reason also, since the day we heard this, we haven't stopped praying for you. We are asking that you may be filled with the knowledge of his will in all wisdom and spiritual understanding, [10] so that you may walk worthy of the Lord, fully pleasing to him: bearing fruit in every good work and growing in the knowledge of God, [11] being strengthened with all power, according to his glorious might, so that you may have great endurance and patience, joyfully [12] giving thanks to the Father, who has enabled you to share in the saints' inheritance in the light.

Week Six

Look back through any notes you made this week as you answer the following questions.

1 What aspects of the Corinthian church surprised you?
What parts of their lives were confusing or different?

2 What teachings from this week's reading challenged you as a member of the body of Christ?

3 How would you like to practice those teachings in your own community this week?

NOTES

Grace

DAY 41

Day

Take this day to catch up on your reading, pray, and rest in the presence of the Lord.

Sow righteousness for yourselves and reap faithful love; break up your unplowed ground. It is time to seek the Lord until he comes and sends righteousness on you like the rain.

HOSEA 10:12

Weekly Truth

Scripture is God-breathed and true. When we memorize it, we carry the good news of Jesus with us wherever we go.

Now that you have finished reading 2 Corinthians, combine your memorization from the last two weeks to remember the entirety of 2 Corinthians 12:9.

But he said to me, "My grace is sufficient for you, for my power is perfected in weakness." Therefore, I will most gladly boast all the more about my weaknesses, so that Christ's power may reside in me.

2 CORINTHIANS 12:9

See tips for memorizing Scripture on page 156.

Be alert, stand
firm in the faith, be
courageous, be strong.
Do everything in love.

1 CORINTHIANS 16:13–14

Tips for Memorizing Scripture

At She Reads Truth, we believe Scripture memorization is an important discipline in your walk with God. Committing God's Truth to memory means He can minister to us—and we can minister to others—through His Word no matter where we are. As you approach the Weekly Truth passage in this book, try these memorization tips to see which techniques work best for you!

STUDY IT

Study the passage in its biblical context and ask yourself a few questions before you begin to memorize it: What does this passage say? What does it mean? How would I say this in my own words? What does it teach me about God? Understanding what the passage means helps you know why it is important to carry it with you wherever you go.

Break the passage into smaller sections, memorizing a phrase at a time.

PRAY IT

Use the passage you are memorizing as a prompt for prayer.

WRITE IT

Dedicate a notebook to Scripture memorization and write the passage over and over again.

Diagram the passage after you write it out. Place a square around the verbs, underline the nouns, and circle any adjectives or adverbs. Say the passage aloud several times, emphasizing the verbs as you repeat it. Then do the same thing again with the nouns, then the adjectives and adverbs.

Write out the first letter of each word in the passage somewhere you can reference it throughout the week as you work on your memorization.

Use a whiteboard to write out the passage. Erase a few words at a time as you continue to repeat it aloud. Keep erasing parts of the passage until you have it all committed to memory.

CREATE

If you can, make up a tune for the passage to sing as you go about your day, or try singing it to the tune of a favorite song.

Sketch the passage, visualizing what each phrase would look like in the form of a picture. Or, try using calligraphy or altering the style of your handwriting as you write it out.

Use hand signals or signs to come up with associations for each word or phrase and repeat the movements as you practice.

SAY IT

Repeat the passage out loud to yourself as you are going through the rhythm of your day—getting ready, pouring your coffee, waiting in traffic, or making dinner.

Listen to the passage read aloud to you.

Record a voice memo on your phone and listen to it throughout the day or play it on an audio Bible.

SHARE IT

Memorize the passage with a friend, family member, or mentor. Spontaneously challenge each other to recite the passage, or pick a time to review your passage and practice saying it from memory together.

Send the passage as an encouraging text to a friend, testing yourself as you type to see how much you have memorized so far.

KEEP AT IT!

Set reminders on your phone to prompt you to practice your passage.

Purchase a She Reads Truth Scripture Card Set or keep a stack of note cards with Scripture you are memorizing by your bed. Practice reciting what you've memorized previously before you go to sleep, ending with the passages you are currently learning. If you wake up in the middle of the night, review them again instead of grabbing your phone. Read them out loud before you get out of bed in the morning.

CSB BOOK ABBREVIATIONS

OLD TESTAMENT

GN Genesis

EX Exodus

LV Leviticus

NM Numbers

DT Deuteronomy

JOS Joshua

JDG Judges

RU Ruth

1SM 1 Samuel

2SM 2 Samuel

1KG 1 Kings

2KG 2 Kings

1CH 1 Chronicles

2CH 2 Chronicles

EZR Ezra

NEH Nehemiah

EST Esther

JB Job

PS Psalms

PR Proverbs

EC Ecclesiastes

SG Song of Solomon

IS Isaiah

JR Jeremiah

LM Lamentations

EZK Ezekiel

DN Daniel

HS Hosea

JL Joel

AM Amos

OB Obadiah

JNH Jonah

MC Micah

NAH Nahum

HAB Habakkuk

ZPH Zephaniah

HG Haggai

ZCH Zechariah

MAL Malachi

NEW TESTAMENT

MT Matthew

MK Mark

LK Luke

JN John

AC Acts

RM Romans

1CO 1 Corinthians

2CO 2 Corinthians

GL Galatians

EPH Ephesians

PHP Philippians

COL Colossians

1TH 1 Thessalonians

2TH 2 Thessalonians

1TM 1 Timothy

2TM 2 Timothy

TI Titus

PHM Philemon

HEB Hebrews

JMS James

1PT 1 Peter

2PT 2 Peter

1JN 1 John

2JN 2 John

3JN 3 John

JD Jude

RV Revelation

BIBLIOGRAPHY

The Book of Common Prayer and Administration of the Sacraments and Other Rites and Ceremonies of the Church.
New York: Church Publishing, Inc., 1789.

Shop the She Reads Truth Online Bookstore

RESOURCES TO HELP YOU READ AND UNDERSTAND GOD'S WORD

Our Online Bookstore is stocked with Daily Reading Guides and supporting resources, available for you to start whenever you're ready. The collection includes guides on books of the Bible, topics that matter, and seasons of the Church calendar. Read on your own, with your church, or with your friends or family, selecting the topic or book you need in each season of your daily reading of God's Word.

IN OUR ONLINE BOOKSTORE YOU'LL FIND

DAILY READING GUIDES

Each of our Daily Reading Guides is available for you to start reading on your own or with your group, whenever you are ready.

BIBLES

Shop our collection of thoughtfully and artfully designed Bibles.

OTHER PRODUCTS

Whether you're looking for books to point your kids toward God through His Word, a curated Bible reading gift set, or apparel that reminds you of truth, we've got just the thing.

SHE READS TRUTH

Shop Now!

SHOPSHEREADSTRUTH.COM

You just spent 42 days in the Word of God!

MY FAVORITE DAY OF
THIS READING PLAN:

ONE THING I LEARNED
ABOUT GOD:

WHAT WAS GOD DOING IN
MY LIFE DURING THIS STUDY?

HOW DID I FIND DELIGHT IN GOD'S WORD?

WHAT DID I LEARN THAT I WANT TO SHARE
WITH SOMEONE ELSE?

A SPECIFIC PASSAGE OR VERSE
THAT ENCOURAGED ME:

A SPECIFIC PASSAGE OR VERSE THAT
CHALLENGED AND CONVICTED ME: